Charis

The Human Voice
of the Holy Bible

Charis

The Human Voice
of the Holy Bible

Mark David Cathcart

BOOKS

Winchester, UK
Washington, USA

First published by O-Books, 2010
O-Books is an imprint of John Hunt Publishing Ltd., The Bothy, Deershot Lodge, Park Lane, Ropley,
Hants, SO24 0BE, UK
office1@o-books.net
www.o-books.com

For distributor details and how to order please visit the 'Ordering' section on our website.

Text copyright: Mark David Cathcart 2010

ISBN: 978 1 84694 356 0

A CIP catalogue record for this book is available from the British Library.

Design: Stuart Davies

Printed in the UK by CPI Antony Rowe
Printed in the USA by Offset Paperback Mfrs, Inc

We operate a distinctive and ethical publishing philosophy in all
areas of our business, from our global network of authors to
production and worldwide distribution.

CONTENTS

The preface of Charis

The psychology of human force that inspired the writings and use of the biblical scriptures

Charis is a humanist response to the decline in church attendance, the readership of the Bible and the role of the Bible and the Church in moral guidance.

For wider interest in the Bible to return a different way of understanding the scriptures might be required, one that operates outside of the belief or non belief syndrome. **Charis** explores the Christian Bible and its traditions from the human perspective rather than from the divine narrative of the Bible itself moving away the traditional interpretation of it by the church and its leaders.

Consistent with the theological content of the Bible throughout, and its historical locations, **Charis** unravels the human motivations that lay behind the original biblical texts, seeking to reveal the genius of human thought that inspired Judaism, Christianity, Catholicism, and eventual agnosticism.

If 'God' is the mystery of how to live as human, our connection to each other and the energy of the universe, as we strive towards our ultimate location and fulfilment, then the Jewish and early Christian texts were indeed striving to understand 'God', a collective expression of how to live and operate initially within the tribe, and later as a spiritual society divorced from politics and state religion.

Charis (ancient Greek): grace, favour, loveliness, kindness

To the memory of Gillian Cathcart

Acknowledgements

The desert bards, the historian scribes, the poets, the songsters, the wisdom makers, the voices of lamentation, the prophetic priesthoods, the resistance writers, the political encoders, the philosopher thinkers, the gospel narrators, the apostolic messengers, the spiritual bloggers, the many thousands combined, the human authors of the holy bible.

The Testaments of Charis

Each of the four testaments of Charis places the composition and use of the biblical texts and the moral guidance they offered in their wider historical setting, in terms of social and leadership structures of the time, and the psychology of thought that these inspired.

The Tribe considers the relationship between the physical, political and social location of the Jews 3000 years ago, and the beliefs and scriptures that these inspired in the Old Testament.

The Soul explores the evolution of early Christianity, a spiritualised version of Judaism inspired by Greek philosophy as a response to Roman oppression, with Jesus and Paul human embodiments of this new faith and its evangelism.

The State examines the genius of political leadership behind Catholicism, with its shrewd combination of Christianity, Judaism and Roman paganism designed to install religious conformity and political control across Europe.

The Individual King considers the eventual separation of religion from politics and the reaction of individuals to their new found religious freedom.

"All scripture is God inspired" Timothy

The Books of Charis

The human evolution of Judaism and Christianity is explored in a sequence of 12 self contained books within each testament.

'Revelation', the final book of each testament, considers the impact at the individual level.

Book	The Tribe	The Soul	The State	The Individual King
1	Deserts	Subjugations	Persecutions	Missions
2	Wars	Martyrs	Gentiles	Trenches
3	Commands	Salvations	Triumphs	Monuments
4	Laws	Spirituals	Romans	Revolutions
5	Sins	Compassions	Devils	Choirs
6	Politics	Philosophies	Politics	Mirrors
7	Races	Psychologies	Popes	Kings
8	Myths	Scribes	Arabs	Merchants
9	Humanities	Locations	Crusaders	Charismatics
10	Expressions	Blogs	Confessions	Therapies
11	Oracles	Letters	Monarchs	Genes
12	Ashes	Humilities	Divisions	Churches
Revelation	Survivors	Challenges	Spires	Charis

Testament 1 The Tribe

The relationship between the physical and social location of the Jews 3000 years ago, and the evolution of their beliefs and scriptures

The books

1	Deserts	5	Sins	9	Humanities
2	Wars	6	Politics	10	Expressions
3	Commands	7	Races	11	Oracles
4	Laws	8	Myths	12	Ashes
Revelation	Survivors				

God for the Jews was the hidden force of the desert protecting the tribe and securing its salvation through victories in war. The laws and customs of the Jews formed their pragmatic way to achieve this, in their quest for God to remain on their side.

Publication of the mythological traditions of the origins of the tribe and its laws were ideal propaganda initially for the kings to control, and later for the priests as they sought to restore tribal order following their Exile in Babylon.

Tales of human emotion, love, betrayal, passion, lust, and revenge brought the law and myth to the personal level. Alongside which were the poetry, and songs of passion, the cultural as well as legal writings of a tribe, seeking survival, and honouring God.

The publication of the prophecies gave the nation hope, but also admonishment to the law breakers, especially those seeking relationships with non Jews.

For survival of the tribe was as much dependent on tradition and custom as territory itself, with the resultant exclusivity of the tribe stronger than any physical demarcation of land.

1 *The Book of Deserts*

The Jews worshipped their god, Jehovah, the invisible force of the desert, desperate to secure land and provision.

Humans formed packs to hunt for food, kill and take territory, and to multiply the tribe. Frustration and fear led to divine creations and worship. Prayers were made to the hidden forces and natural elements of the land and sea in their bid to control the weather and secure the harvest.

Human emotions, passions and lusts, became gods, divine forces of intelligence, war, and love, living high up in the mountains above the clouds driving humans to act. Humans on the earth below stooped in worship, offered their sacrifices and looked for signs, hoping for a better outcome.

The Jews were the desert tribe, nomads preoccupied with territory and provision, desert wanderers, worshipping a divine force to protect them from their enemies, defeat them in battle, and provide them with the 'milk and honey', and the 'promised land'. Their god was the hidden and whispering voice of the desert, amid the wandering stars and shifting sands. Fearing their god would abandon them for another desert tribe, the Jews proffered themselves in worship and honour to show their loyalty.

Evolution of local tribes into one Jewish federation demanded one God of Israel, Jehovah. Regional gods all made way for Jehovah to secure loyalty and protection, and victory in battle, a powerful force that supported them in defence against attack, and their attack on foreign soil. Jehovah was a god to be feared, worshipped and appeased by sacrifice, a god that could secure their territory, and save the nation.

The desert wanderers slept on the desert sands, stars shining in the blackness of the night, holes to Heaven, God's residence where he heard their prayers, received their sacrifices and watched over his people, the Jews.

"I will make of you a great nation, and I will bless you" Exodus

2 The Book of Wars

God was the divine force of protection for the Jews as they fought to defend their territory, their lord of hosts as they sought to extend it.

God was the overseer of the Jews, their protector against invaders, the divine force that established them land after their desert wanderings, the inspiration behind the fall of the walls of Jericho. God was their lord of hosts, the hidden power that determined success or failure in battle, the conquering force that laid Canaan to waste, with extermination of all who lived in it.

The walls of Jericho came down and the Canaanites fell to their deaths. Jehovah was a God of war, with his role as a God of love limited to one nation only, the Jews.

God was a king on his throne in a court in the Heavens, with the Jews his subjects, in supplication and prayer for his favour, grace and mercy. Success in battle depended on whether God's favour had been secured, with God an instrument of vengeance and jealousy, who loved his people provided they loved him. Salvation of the nation depended on successful worship of God, none more so than in war.

God gave courage to the Jews when they faced enemies larger than their own, urged them not to be afraid of their horses and chariots. Enemies, the Hittites, the Amorites, the Canaanites, the Perizzites, the Hivites and the Jebusites deserved annihilation. Males were put to the sword, females and children taken as booty. There was no mercy; Saul's failure to destroy the Amalekites was scorned by God and his army.

The Jews needed land and provision with God on their side in the attack justifying their advance.

1000 BC and the Jews rejoiced. David had defeated the Philistines with Jerusalem established as the seat of Jewish power. The nation was expanding, the aggressor and the victor in battle and war. God was on their side, and the Jews gave thanks.

"But as for the towns of these people that the Lord is giving you as an inheritance, you must not let anything that breathes remain alive."
Deuteronomy

3 The Book of Commandments

Salvation of the nation was dependent on keeping to the tribal rules.

As long as the Jews behaved according to the law, God would provide with land and provisions, and lead the nation to salvation and glory. Application of the law formed their moral code, their religious way of life, to secure what was best for the tribe, their Covenant with God.

The Law of Moses was the rule book for Jewish society, how to live as citizens, their rights to livelihood and property, punishments for failure to comply, a corporation employment manual ostensibly for the rights and comfort of the employees, but for nothing more than the furtherance of the corporation itself.

From sexual relations to the harvesting of fruit from a tree, this was the law of the land at the micro and macro level, with

God the legal foundation. Divine and secular rules had no distinction. Secular was divine, and God was the law.

The Ten Commandments formed the base, handed down by Jewish tradition from God to Moses at a time when the tribes were still wandering the desert, following their escape from captivity in Egypt. The Jews were soon to settle in Canaan, with the Jewish nation requiring for the first time a structured set of rules for society to function.

God was the protector. The greatest risk was for God to be offended and abandon the nation, with the first four commandments reflecting this fear, the first to worship God only, and no other gods.

Later troubles that afflicted the nation, the fall of Jerusalem and Exile to Babylon, were blamed squarely on the worshipping of idols, the second of the commandments, and God abandoning them as punishment. Loyalty to God was the key to the nation's survival, with a further commandment not to take God's name in vain. To honour God, the Sabbath was to be kept holy.

The remainder of the commandments were more applicable to any social grouping; not to murder, not to bear false witness, not to thieve, not to steal a wife, the property of the husband. The Ten Commandments were for a society where demarcations of ownership were important, where honouring parents and family was key, and where trust in God formed the core.

"the Lord summoned Moses to the top of the mountain, and Moses went up" Exodus

4 The Book of Laws

A corporation rule book was established, a pragmatic approach to community living, reflecting the social needs of a tribe seeking its own advancement.

More specific rules followed, on sacrifice, sex, diet, harvest, sickness based on a clear and well founded pragmatism, with health, well being and survival of the nation the goal. The removal of lepers to the outside of the town to prevent further contamination; excuse from military service in the first year of marriage to encourage procreation; avoidance of pork and red meat to avoid contamination in a hot climate; prohibition on charging interest on loans between members of the tribes to promote the wealth of the nation as a whole rather than any one individual; not harvesting the fruit of the tree in the initial years of growth to secure better yield for the future; giving the blood and entrails of animal sacrifice so the Jews could feast on the meat.

The law was a quest for order rather than vengeance, 'eye for eye' and 'tooth for tooth' that punishment should be measured according to the crime, rather than a process of vengeance that could escalate. A range of punishments for breaking the commandments and rules were set out. Stoning was the common form of execution, the number of lashes set at 40. With God the foundation of the law, blasphemers were stoned to death.

Adultery was deemed theft, with the wife owned by the husband, to protect property rights and legacies. A Jewish male could sleep with his slaves, and have concubines, but faced the death penalty if he slept with the wife of another Jew. Bastard offspring were inheritance outcasts, with an illicit union affecting the family for 10 generations, banned from the Assembly of God. Rapists faced death, with the victim of the rape excused if she was in the country unable to summon help, stoned if in the city.

Slaves were a possession. The law permitted the hitting of slaves with a rod, provided they survived for two days after the beating. Some degree of brutality was permitted, but owners were also reminded that the Jews were once captive in Egypt, with some compassion required.

The law was structured at all levels to secure a growing population, strong and able to defend against enemy attack and secure land and provision for its members.

Provision for the sick was limited, with spread of disease the key concern; the disabled were outcasts.

Religious ceremony was at the heart of society, and the blemished, the dwarfs and the deformed were all banned from the offering of God's food, with lepers prohibited from eating sacrificial donations. Deference to the old was encouraged to embrace the wisdom that their age offered to the community.

Love your neighbour as yourself was the core precept of living among the Jews. But the definition of neighbour was tightly defined. Neighbours were limited to members of the Jewish nation who were healthy, able to participate fully in the functions of religious and community living, and contribute to the group. There was no compassion for enemies, limited sympathy for slaves, and no room for lepers or the 'unclean'.

Purification was essential, with blood defilement. Females were unclean during menstruation. Male and female were both unclean after the birth of their baby, demanding an unblemished lamb be sacrificed.

Tattoos were not permitted and hair was to be cut off at the temples.

The law was a pragmatic approach towards the health and successful multiplication of its people. God was at its core with observation to detail and obsessive cleanliness designed to secure his favour. The law was full of superstitions, driven by the need to keep God with the nation.

"eye for eye, tooth for tooth, hand for hand, foot for foot" Leviticus

5 *The Book of Sins*

Sin and law were defined by the community needs.

The Covenant was God's rule book, faithfulness to it essential if the Jewish nation was to prosper. A good man kept to the law, a sinful man broke it, with sin regarded as any action that broke the Covenant, and disadvantaged the community.

Achan stole the gold sacred to God with the Jews losing their next battle for Canaan; the path of the individual affected the entire nation.

The challenge for the individual was to avoid the sinful urges that might stand in the way of the progression of the nation as a whole.

It was man's nature to be sinful, the story of Adam and Eve, the apple of knowledge, the beguiling serpent and the eviction from Eden. The fall of Adam was man's challenge to overcome sin, and to abide by God's principles.

Man had learnt to communicate, and knew how other people felt; he had eaten the apple. But he also needed food, territory, and a mate to breed, driven by passion and desire, beguiled by the serpent. Conscience stood in the way, how much to take at the expense of others.

For the Jews the Covenant was the answer to their conscience. God was their guiding force, who justified their taking, and protected them from enemy forces encroaching on their territory.

The Covenant with God and law was a code of behaviour that at times demanded the death and destruction of non Jews, or even Jews within the community, those that had broken the law, or the sick and infirm, but always looked to the benefit of the Jewish community as a whole.

There was no sin in casting away the lepers, stoning a law breaker, or taking the females of a captured city as booty and young children as slaves. But there was sin if a Jew had sex with the wife of another Jew, failed to put to the sword the males of the enemy, or allowed a leper to participate in the food of sacrifice.

God demanded justice, with any action which broke the Covenant a sin not only against the Jewish nation, but against God himself. The Jewish nation was on a quest to take the 'right' path, away from sin, to retain God's favour, and for the nation to survive.

"Then the Lord said to Cain, 'Where is your brother Abel?'" Genesis

6 The Book of Politics

By claiming that the Law of Moses was handed down directly from God himself the new kingship could claim divine validation of the rules it imposed on the nation.

The judges that had formerly gathered as tribe representatives during moments of crisis finally united under one king to combat the Philistines. David's kingship in the wake of his defeat of the Philistines marked the change, with federal rules required for the previously independent tribes and families.

The king's role needed validating, as the lynch pin of society, enforcer of the law, and most importantly mediator between the Jewish people and God.

For the first time, a human was adopting messianic status, closer to the divine, holding authority over the entire nation. The king could claim God as the higher force that gave the laws, and thereby demand that society obey them. The relation between king and his people was made easier as a result. The king, after all, was not the absolute authority, but the servant of the law instated by God, with the people servants to the king, and ultimately God.

Secular and divine laws were thereby one and the same, with

David, and the kings that followed him, the human connector with God.

The new Jewish kingship formalised the traditional histories of the tribes by publishing the stories of Moses, a move to support the kingship constitution, and the laws that it represented. When Athens adopted democracy 500 years later a wealth of Greek mythological literature was published exploring the moral precepts on which this democracy was founded. 500 years later still when Rome moved to an imperial regime under Augustus, Virgil's Aeneid was published, the story of Rome's mythological origins and connections to Troy. The Jews set the trend, validating the law and political system, with myth published as fact.

Genesis, Exodus, Leviticus, Numbers and Deuteronomy were formulated, pulling together historical and mythological strands. Collectively they expounded the early formation of the tribes: God's special love for them as they escaped Egypt towards the promised land of Canaan; the establishment of God's commandments and laws along the way, handed directly by God to Moses on tablets of stone; the Ark of the Covenant that transported them through their years of desert wanderings.

The king required his people to follow his leadership. The Pentateuch, these five books, achieved this, teaching the people of God's role in establishing the laws that David represented. Myth was written as fact, with God loving the Jews throughout. David's kingship was the pinnacle of this love, with his role as the victor over the Philistines, the slayer of Goliath.

Jerusalem was the new 'promised land', the Temple a physical sign of God's authority over his people and David's kingship over the nation.

"I took you from the pasture, from following sheep to be prince over my people Israel" Samuel

7 The Book of Races

Following the return of the Jews from Exile, the scriptures were formally published, with racial purity the new dominating theme.

Jerusalem had fallen to the Babylonians at the beginning of the sixth century BC, with the Temple of Solomon destroyed. The majority of the nation was forced to live in Babylon in the decades that followed.

Xerxes the Persian defeated the Babylonians some 60 years later, at which point the Jews were free to return to Jerusalem if they wished. Although some chose to stay behind, many chose to return to rebuild the Temple of Jerusalem.

The event of Exile now dominated the writings of the Jews. The books of Ezra and Nehemiah narrated the return of the Jews to Jerusalem and the Temple rebuild, with the book of Lamentations a collective expression of the nation's sorrow at their period in Exile. The extensive writings of the prophets, Isaiah, Jeremiah, and Ezekiel predicted the Jewish Exile in Babylon and the re-emergence of a new Jewish state thereafter.

If the millennium proceeding, from the initial years of settling in Canaan to the defeat of the Philistines, had been the foundation of the Jewish nation, the return from Exile was its defining moment. Part of the Jewish tribe was now living abroad, in Babylon or elsewhere. Geography was no longer the boundary that defined the race, with tighter customs and beliefs required to compensate.

Ezra imposed the edict banning marriage to non Jews, demanding divorce from foreign wives in the process. Ruth the mother of David was a non Jew; she had married Boaz and adopted the Jewish customs. But this precedent appeared discounted, with Nehemiah describing the marriages of Solomon to non Jews as a great sin. The Jewish race was closing ranks, with purity of blood its defining territory, as much as the walls of any Temple, or geographical boundaries of any city or country.

Religion was now at the heart of the nation's fabric with the priests not the kings in charge. To indoctrinate the Jewish nation the scriptures were properly formalised.

A new history was composed, Chronicles, alongside the earlier recordings of the nation's history contained within Joshua, Judges, Ruth, Samuel and Kings.

Chronicles special focus was on genealogy, with the generations of the various tribes listed in detail to underline the importance now being attached to racial purity. The extensive writings of the prophets were also rationalised, adjusted to sit neatly with actual events, with the additional prophesy of a new golden age for the race added, the hope of a new Messianic David to return the Jews to an age of glory.

Insecurity dominated the scriptures; how had the tribe upset God, why the Exile, and what could be done to prevent it in the future. The answer was clear. If the Jews, whether inside the walls of Jerusalem or far away in Babylon, adhered to the traditions, customs and laws of their ancestors, inspired by their forefathers Jacob, Israel, Abraham and Moses, and remained faithful to God, the nation would survive.

In the post Exile period understanding of the scriptures and the keeping of its law were now synonymous with the survival of the nation itself. Daily the scriptures were read aloud from the steps of the Temple, with the law of the Jewish nation embedded deep into its psychology.

The territory of the Jewish nation was now defined by the pickets and fences of laws on subsistence, rules of sexual reproduction, codes of the work place, and political and sociological frameworks. Geographical boundaries were important, and the Jews would continue to defend Jerusalem; but the survival of the nation was no longer dependent on territory alone.

"All these had married foreign women, and they sent them away with their children" Nehemiah

8 The Book of Myths

The nation's myth was compiled into historic sequence, to inspire future generations to remain true to God and the Jewish nation.

The scribes committed to papyrus the oral traditions of the bards. Events had been relayed from one generation to the next, embellished with heroism and fantasy along the way, Noah's ark to save life on earth, the staff of Moses to part the seas, David's sling to slay Goliath. This rich tapestry of myth was carefully slotted into place by the scribes, constructed into a seamless historical line to explain the early roots of the Jewish people, their special relationship with God, and the need to keep his law.

God rewarded faithfulness; righteous Noah was therefore God's chosen to build the ark. God protected lineage; Jacob's birth right was robbed by Esau, but reinstated by God. God protected his people; Joseph was robbed of his multi coloured coat, but rewarded with status. God rewarded faithfulness; Isaac had bound his son for sacrifice, as God had commanded, but the son was spared, with the Jewish nation born as a consequence. The scribes incorporated bard myth into the official scriptures for the Jewish nation to read. Keep the Covenant, and God will reward, as he rewarded Noah, Jacob and Joseph.

Generation upon generation of children of the Jewish tribe listened beneath the desert stars spell bound by Exodus, the images of sinking chariots, and drowning Egyptians, the sea cascading over the army in pursuit of the Jews.

The sequence of plagues, the rivers of blood, the frogs, the boils, and the pestilence, and the predictability of pharaoh's defiance on each occasion, until the final unfolding of the death of the first born, mesmerised them. Exodus was a monument to the nation's will to survive captivity, a core energy of scripture designed to sustain the belief of the Jewish people that God would not forsake them, however bad it got.

Exodus was also the mythical narrative of a nation coming of age, the tribe on a desert journey, to find its true spiritual location, learning the values of a new society to sustain them for generations to come.

Moses received the commandments from God, but the tribe worshipped the golden calf instead, with the 'promised land' proving allusive until the Jews learnt to trust God properly. Odysseus in the Greek epic poem The Odyssey relied on his intelligence to find his way home; Aeneas, in the Roman epic poem The Aeneid, relied on his sense of duty to found Rome. Greeks were intelligent philosophers, Romans dutiful soldiers, Jews a people of faith. For the Jews to find their new homeland, faithfulness to God was required, with their wanderings in the desert their journey towards faithfulness.

"Then the Lord said to Moses 'Go to Pharaoh and say to him, "Thus says the Lord: Let my people go, so that they may worship me'" Exodus

9 The Book of Humanities

King and subjects were all open to sin and punishment from God, with tales of court intrigue to entertain with their stories of love, betrayal, passion, lust, and revenge.

Beyond the great stories of myth, and between the narratives of court and battle, as the leaders vied for power and authority, and the Jewish armies gained and lost territory, lay stories of human emotion, tales of love, hate, friendship, betrayal, courage, and jealousy.

David the young warrior killed Goliath, sealing a close bond of friendship with Jonathan, King Saul's younger son. Their friendship led to Jonathan working against his father to secure David's safety. For David to be safe, Jonathan had to let David go, with the narrative of David and Jonathan embracing for the last time an eternal portrayal of friendship and love.

David's success in battle, meanwhile, led to the jealousy of King Saul; the king had formal leadership over his people, but had been usurped by a talented subordinate whose charisma generated the greater power of the two. Through tricks and challenges Saul attempted to end David's life but failed. David in return had opportunities to kill Saul but decided not to, keeping the moral high ground. Saul committed suicide.

David was made king, anointed by God, his lineage enjoying a special Covenant with the lord of hosts. Yet, like the rest of the tribe, David had sinned, falling short of the challenge to keep to God's rule book. He saw Bathsheba bathing, looking at her beauty from the roof, and yielded to his desire, committing adultery and breaking the commandment of Moses.

Worse still, David murdered her husband, by ensuring his death in battle. David was full of remorse, but God gave his punishment, the death of their first born son.

If the story of Exodus was big screen entertainment, the stories of David formed the soap, portrayals of human nature, and the struggle of man to avoid acts of selfish gain that hurt others. David recognised his sin with Bathsheba, just as Saul recognised his sin against David, despite which, both went ahead and sinned in any case.

The Jewish scriptures set out the laws of God, and then enacted them not only at the individual level, but at the highest levels in society. No-one was immune. All members of the tribe were human, open to sin, and to punishment from God.

"David saw the woman bathing from the roof; she was very beautiful"
Kings

10 The Book of Expressions

Verses of poetic song, passion and wisdom were composed and shared at public recitations.

A sequence of books followed the texts of historical narrative expressing the personal sentiments of those living through these periods: love and despair in Psalms, common sense in Proverbs, realism in Ecclesiastes, and passion in Song of Solomon. Their combination expressed timeless sentiments, appealing to the deepest understandings of love and grief, hope and despair, passion and emptiness.

They were preceded by the fable of Job, the story of a man tested by God with a number of hardships, his life crushed by financial loss, poor health, and the loss of loved ones; he endured to the end though, rewarded by God for his faithfulness. The overriding theme as always was the need for a nation's faithfulness; however bad it got, God would remain true to his people provided they kept faith with him. Job brought this to the personal level, with extended expressions of Job's personal despair, but also his endurance. This set the tone for the books of personal expression that followed.

The sentiments expressed were universal, with specifics rarely mentioned, and formed a body of literature that explored the range of emotions, thoughts on how to behave, and wider views on the meaning of life.

The psalms were poetic, laden with metaphor and image, rhythmic, appealing to melody, with simple expressions that conveyed love, hope, despair, regret, remorse. Proverbs lacked the legalistic and proscriptive approach of the earlier commandments and laws included in the histories, musing in their nature, common sense in their delivery with wider appeal and relevance. Ecclesiastes was universal, the pointlessness of life, the seasons of time, and the importance of wisdom but also its limitation given the wider forces at play. Song of Solomon was love poetry, sensuous in design, pure and simple, with language and images of love, passion and desire.

The context of these books was that of a Jewish people at an individual and cultural level, seeking God to show them love, give them land and defend them against their enemies, the content of Psalms, on condition that they keep His laws and Covenant, as set out in Proverbs. The limitation of the human condition was recognised, the theme of Ecclesiastes, but the hope of the nation's survival through the joy of personal love and procreation, poeticised in Song of Solomon, compensated.

"Make haste, my beloved, and be like a gazelle or a young stag upon the mountains of spices" Song of Solomon

11 The Book of Oracles

The prophets gave the Jews hope of a new age of glory to come, blaming the nation's decline on foreign influence.

The Greeks consulted the oracle on matters of military and state importance; Assyria had shouters and revellers; and the Jews had their prophets, men who would receive visions and messages from God.

The prophets mainly lived in the ninth to sixth centuries BC, with their prophecies mostly related to events that took place towards the end of this period, the fall of Israel to the Assyrians, of Judah to Babylon, and the eventual return from Exile and rebuild of the Temple. There was also a forward reference to a new Messianic force that would come after the return from Exile, a second King David, the restorer of the Jewish nation to its former glory.

The opening sentence of each book of prophecy declared the name of the prophet and dated the prophecy by naming the king of the time. This dating device therefore gave the appearance if not the reality that many of the events being predicted did indeed take place after the prophecy had been made. Isaiah predicted Assyria's move into Israel. Given that Isaiah lived after Israel's fall this was a prediction after the event. But his writings also predicted the later period of Jewish Exile in Babylon, with Isaiah living before this event. These later writings were, like so many of the prophetic passages, neatly doctored by Ezra and his team of scribes in the late sixth century BC, with predictions and eventual outcomes matched.

A core purpose of the books of the prophets, more important perhaps than the predictions themselves, was to bring people back to obedience.

With a sequence of images and metaphor in the form of ecstatic poetry the prophets outlined Judah's decline, and the failure of the Jewish people to keep to God's Covenant. The nation was a harlot corrupted by foreign influence, a whore that entertained foreign idols, a faithless bride, fornicator of foreign gods and religion, a valley of dry bones that one day would regain flesh and return to Zion.

The prophetic writings were a medium whereby the priests of the Jewish nation could bring the people to heel with admonishments, and reminders of what could happen if the law was not kept, if the religious traditions were let go, if the people became 'less Jewish'. The prophet books were a goad to keep the Jews Jewish. But with a carrot attached: keep to the law, and a new Messiah would come, with Judah restored to its former glory.

"O dry bones, hear the word of the Lord" Ezekiel

12 The Book of Ashes

Jews were faithful to God to secure the safety and prosperity of the nation not because they believed in an afterlife.

As a nomadic tribe, and later as a nation with walls and borders, the key preoccupation was the survival of the tribe from attack and slaughter from invaders, and survival of the individuals within the tribe from famine, and disease. Multiplication of the tribe through procreation was essential. The laws and precepts of the scriptures were synonymous with the survival of the Jewish nation, and the family line.

The Jewish scriptures were not about life after death of the individual, but life of the tribe after the death of the individual. At times this meant the necessary shortening of individual lives to secure this, with limited provision made for the sick or unclean; the tribe would survive better with the sick removed to avoid contagion. The tribe always came first.

On the rare occasions where the after-death was mentioned, it was described as a shadowy state beneath the earth. Only few escaped this, Enoch and Elijah, who sat with God in Heaven. The individual Jew would not expect to join God in Heaven after death, and would not live his life according to the scriptures in the hope of achieving this. Faithfulness to the scriptures meant that God would remain faithful to the tribe, and support the nation against attack.

Blood to the Jews was the life force; there was no concept of soul. The spilling of blood during the sacrifice of animals was nothing more than the yielding of the life to God. Conversely, the spilling or sharing of blood between Jews was to be avoided at all costs, as was the eating of red meat. When the blood stopped flowing, life had gone, and that was it; there was no soul to float up to Heaven.

"you are dust, and to dust you shall return" Genesis

The Revelation of Survivors

The scriptures forged the psychology of the nation, to survive even if territory was lost.

The Jews were a tribe like any other, a collection of individuals seeking safety and efficiency in numbers to ward off threats, gain territory and become stronger.

Like all tribes the Jews had customs and religion, sacrifices and a temple, ways of living together and rules to knit the group and grant identity. Like all nations, the Jews had their history, battling their neighbours, enjoying their victories and suffering their defeats. Like all cultures in the region the Jews had their scriptures and myths.

Specifically the Jews believed that their God Jehovah loved them to the exclusion of all others. God was their spiritual embodiment, their heart, and their faithfulness, the very essence of what it meant to be a Jew. Survival of the nation was dependent on God's special love for them, provided they kept to God's law, God's Covenant with his people.

The Jewish nation flourished for centuries, supported by the teachings of the Pentateuch, and the physical presence of the Temple building.

Following defeat and Exile to Babylon the Jews clung to the hope provided by the prophets of an age of prosperity to come, a new Messiah, a second King David to regenerate the nation. Provided the tribe remained racially pure, the Jews would survive even if they lost Jerusalem, forced abroad as out casts.

"Israel saw the great work that the Lord did against the Egyptians. So the people feared the Lord, and believed in the Lord and his servant Moses." Exodus

Testament 11 The Soul

Christianity the spiritual response to the oppression of Rome with its internalisation of Judaism inspired by Greek philosophy

The books

1	Subjugations	5	Compassions	9	Locations
2	Martyrs	6	Philosophies	10	Blogs
3	Salvations	7	Psychologies	11	Letters
4	Spirituals	8	Scribes	12	Humilities
Revelation	Challenges				

The Jews suffered a sequence of foreign invasions and for lengthy periods were forced to abandon their customs. Stories of Daniel were composed as an inspired resistance, with Daniel a super hero remaining true to the Jewish custom even if it meant death.

Influenced by Greek philosophy, one sect went further, internalising Judaism altogether. The religious system for the state was replaced by a spiritual system for the individual, with the offer of eternal life.

Co-incident to the revolt of the Jews against the Romans in the middle part of the first century AD, and their later eviction from Jerusalem, the Christian movement compiled their narratives of inspiration, with Jesus replacing Daniel as the new super hero.

Jesus was the human embodiment of Christianity, with stories surrounding him to match the faith, woven together as narratives to form the gospel story. Christian tracts were also published in the form of letters, with Paul's missionary an allegory of the spread of this new spirituality.

Christianity had been formed as a direct response to the brutality of Rome with its message of love and compassion, and as a challenge to the intransigence of Judaism with its inclusion of Jews and non Jews alike. It was a spiritual system programmed for success.

1 The Book of Subjugations

A sequence of imperial incursions culminated in the Jews losing Jerusalem, with Christianity emerging as its spiritual replacement.

One page separated the last book of the Old Testament Jewish scriptures, Malachi, from the first book of the New Testament Christian writings, Matthew.

Yet with one turn of the page God had transformed from a warrior God of Israel to a God of love for the world, with no warning at all. God was not about to change, according to Malachi, warning the Jews not to marry outside their race. Yet in Matthew God was suddenly open to all, Jews and non Jews alike, with salvation of the individual rather than the Jewish state the goal.

The Jews had returned from Babylon to Jerusalem in the late 6th century BC, successfully rebuilding their Temple, and reasserting their culture and customs with the core of the scriptures published in the decades that followed.

By the time Matthew was composed 500 years later, however, the Jews were in the last throes of losing it all with the destruction of the Temple by the Romans, and the expulsion of the Jews from Jerusalem.

The Greeks came first, with Palestine under the control of Ptolemy by the early fourth century BC. The Jews were allowed to keep their faith, though with the strict boundaries of their religion under pressure from the more philosophical and exploratory thinking of the Greeks.

A considerably more serious threat emerged in the second century BC, however, with the Syrians taking control. The walls of Jerusalem were destroyed, with the Temple desecrated and the death penalty imposed on those practising the Jewish faith. Rebellions followed, in response to the Syrians participating in sacrifices illegitimate to the Jewish traditions, with Jewish victory achieved in 160 BC.

A new golden age of Judaism emerged, albeit short lived, as a hundred years later Palestine became part of the Roman Empire with the Jews subjugated to the Romans. Their cruelty led to the first Jewish war. Jerusalem was levelled to the ground by the Romans as a response, with the Jews banned from entering the city altogether. The city was rebuilt by Hadrian in Roman tradition, with a temple built to Jupiter at its centre.

Throughout the 500 year stretch between Malachi and Matthew, the Jews had encountered the Greeks, and the Syrians, and survived them both. The Romans marked the end, however, Jerusalem for the Jews no more, with pockets of the tribe forced to live in other countries.

Survival of the Jewish nation was now solely dependent on its rituals and customs and racial purity being properly maintained in these overseas communities.

There was one group of Jews that stood apart, however, adopting a more spiritual response to the brutality of Rome, internalising the faith, adapting Judaism to the works of the Greek philosophers. The Book of Matthew and the New Testament scriptures that followed was their written response, and marked the beginnings of the Christian faith inspired by the centuries of suffering that had preceded it.

"'Do you see these great buildings? Not one stone will be left here upon another; all will be thrown down.'" Mark

Charis

2 The Book of Martyrs

Stories of defiance were composed during the Syrian invasion, with Daniel the super hero to inspire martyrdom.

The Syrians took control of Jerusalem in the second century BC. With Judaism outlawed it was up to the individual to remain faithful to God and the Jewish law.

Jews continued to write during this difficult period, with words contained within their Apocryphal writings encouraging defiance even martyrdom. The Apocrypha was a sequence of Jewish books the bulk of which were composed between the time frame of publications of the Old and New Testaments. The spiritual link between Judaism and early Christianity was being formed, the judgemental God of Israel transforming into the gracious God of Jesus, with the Apocryphal writings an expression of it.

Stories of Daniel were composed to encourage defiance at a time when the Jews were being forced to participate in illegitimate sacrifice and worship.

The historical placement of Daniel was not the current Syrian situation, but the court of Nebuchadnezzar in Babylon during Jewish Exile some 400 years before, with pressure on Daniel to participate in non Jewish worship.

Daniel was the human embodiment of the frustrated uprising of the Jewish spirit in the face of Syrian control. Rather than write directly against the Syrians, and risk death as a consequence, the Jewish scribes created Daniel as an allegory of defiance. Daniel refused to participate in foreign religious practice, or to recognise other gods, and was fed to the lions as punishment. Although judged guilty by the court of man, he was innocent under God, and saved, with the lions tamed.

Daniel was the superhero of the time, with other Daniel stories to inspire. Daniel saved Susanna from execution in the face of her

26

faithfulness to God. Daniel escaped execution for proving to the king that the god Bel was not real. Daniel escaped the lions once more for killing a dragon that the Babylonians worshipped as a god.

These stories and more proved the perfect antidote for the Jewish people in oppression, coerced into religious practice profane to their beliefs. Daniel lived up to his name, 'God my Judge'. The Jews needed to remain true to their God, if any uprising was to succeed, with God, rather than a foreign leader or ideology, their judge.

In the earlier scriptures, Jews were willing to face death in battle for no other purpose than to support the survival of the nation. But now, in Daniel, with the nation already oppressed, there was a new reward to attack when all seemed lost, an afterlife in Heaven. With martyrdom an encouraged response, the Jewish authors of Daniel wrote of an afterlife for the wise and righteous. Daniel's vision, written more than 300 years after the rest of the Old Testament scriptures were finalised, was the first time where the notion of an afterlife was being properly entertained in the Jewish scriptures.

Defiance in the face of death and the promise of an afterlife in Heaven formed the core to the Apocryphal writings, peace and immortality for the righteous suffering torments and torture, with a chilling episode of martyrdom to close.

Seven brothers had been tortured and put to death by a tyrant for refusing to eat defiled food. Despite being beaten with scourges, racked on the wheel, and burnt by flames, the sons spoke defiance, claiming loyalty to Abraham. The youngest son left until last was offered clemency if he ate the food. On the encouragement of his mother, he refused, and together they jumped into the flames, with purity of soul, immortality, and a place in Heaven with their ancestors their reward for martyrdom.

"'O Daniel, servant of the living God, has your God whom you faithfully serve been able to deliver you from the lions?'" Daniel

3 The Book of Salvations

The Roman oppression that followed demanded something more, with Jesus, the super hero of eternal life, supplanting Daniel.

Daniel in the Apocrypha was the figure of defiance, true to God, risking death. But Jesus in the New Testament writings that followed went further; he was the offer of salvation himself, the promise of eternal life, the reward in Heaven for Daniel-like defiance. Jesus was the New Testament version of Joshua who led the tribe out of the desert into the 'promised land' of Jericho, now leading the individual to the promised land of eternity.

Jesus in Greek, Joshua in Hebrew, both lived up to their names 'God saves', God saving the individual by Jesus, just as 'God saved' the Jewish nation by Joshua.

Daniel, 'God my judge', had been eclipsed by Jesus, 'God saves', the central character of an emerging Jewish sect, the Christians, equipped with a growing collection of stories of a man with the power to save in the current period of oppression, with meaning and purpose for those now suffering under Roman rule.

Jesus disrupted the money traders in the Temple, with his claim to be the son of God, heresy to the Jewish community. Like Daniel, he faced certain death, endured torture, thorns embedded into his scalp, his skin torn by the lash and scourge. Nails were hammered into his hands and feet, with his body hung vertically, impaled on a cross, struggling to breath, taken for dead, like Daniel entering the lions' den.

Jesus went beyond the earlier stories of Daniel, however, and offered something more. Daniel had always survived. Jesus not only died, he came back from the dead.

Daniel demonstrated the internal conviction required to secure eternal life; Jesus demonstrated eternal life itself. Jesus was the saviour, with salvation no longer the survival of the Jewish nation, but the soul of the individual from sin.

Jesus was the new character of aspiration with stories of defiance, and loyalty to God in the face of death, but also the powers of healing, salvation, and Resurrection from death to an afterlife.

Jesus was an antidote not just to the communities in Jerusalem but anywhere buckling under Roman rule, with traditional Judaism having little to offer in the face of imperial brutality. Jesus offered internal spirituality and an afterlife to come.

"'Why do you look for the living among the dead? He is not here, but has risen'" Luke

4 The Book of Spirituals

The Jews lost Jerusalem and their Temple of worship, with the revolutionary response of Christianity no longer requiring the external trappings of religion.

Judaism was the Jews' relationship with their own God, and worship and honour of him, to secure the salvation and advantage of the Jewish state over their enemies. Christianity operated in a different sphere, personal salvation, and the relationship of the individual with God rather than society as a whole. Christianity moved away from the state towards the individual, a response to Judaism's political decline.

Jews were forced to abandon their open worship, first under

the Syrians, later under the Romans. The Jewish uprising in AD 70 ended in defeat and humiliation, with the Temple destroyed, and the Jewish leaders forced to participate in a humiliating triumphal procession in Rome. The remnants of the uprising were slaughtered at Masada. With no Temple, and no priesthood, the rabbi teachers had become the voice of Judaism, but with different opinions on how to respond.

The response of the Christian Jews to the climate of political oppression was to let go of the physical trappings of religion and focus on an internal spirituality with God. Christian Jews no longer needed a physical Temple. God who resided in the Temple now lived in the body of the Christian, with the body the Temple of God.

The sacrifice to appease God that took place in the Temple, now took place inside the Christian body, as it 'drunk' the blood of Jesus and 'ate' his body. Rather than animal blood shed at the altar, Jesus' blood was shed inside the Christian. Sins were forgiven no longer via the medium of the priest at the Temple, but via personal prayer through the Son of God. The Holy Spirit of God breathed inside the Christian, no longer inside the Temple.

What Jews could no longer do publicly, with their Temple destroyed Christian Jews could now conduct internally, according to the spiritual systems of the New Testament. According to the gospel story, Jesus died on the crucifix, with the veil of the Temple immediately ripped into two; the holy of holies the sacred area where before only the high priest had been granted access was revealed; access to God for the Christian was direct, via the death of Jesus and his subsequent Resurrection. The formal religious system had been torn to shreds.

God's Covenant with the Jewish people was now a Covenant with the individual. The process whereby God saved the Jewish state in return for their devotion and faithfulness as a race was now redundant, with personal salvation dependent on individual devotion and love. The Jewish Passover, the celebration of the State's liberation from slavery, required sacrifice of a perfect animal, a lamb; in contrast, holy communion and the Last Supper was now celebrated to commemorate the individual's liberation from the slavery of sin, the sacrifice of a perfect human, Jesus, the lamb of God.

The priest, the Temple and the sacrifice were all replaced by a spiritual system that now operated within the individual, the prophets of the nation, their admonishments of the present, and predictions for the future, also gone, replaced by the Holy Spirit that now lived inside the individual Christian, guided their actions, gave them the power to prophesy in tongues.

The Jewish state of Jerusalem had been crushed by the Romans, with Hadrian burying the foundations of the Jewish Temple under the buildings, arcades and temples of a new Rome. But the Jewish system for the Christian Jews survived in a non physical, spiritual form that lived in the hearts of its members. The scribes, the priests, the rabbis, even the law itself had been replaced by God's agent Jesus the personal judge, and saviour.

Judaism was the state, with salvation of the nation dependent on keeping to the law, remaining faithful to God. Multiplication of the race, and participation in Jewish society was its citizenship. Christianity in contrast was the individual keeping to God's love, and remaining faithful to Jesus, spreading God's message of love and sharing personal gifts of the spirit within the community.

"They were astounded at his teaching, for he taught them as one having authority, and not as the scribe" Luke

5 The Book of Compassions

**Rome was a society based on the sword and brutality, with
Christianity compassionate and pacifist in return.**

Roman culture was enmeshed in pagan traditions, a military
culture based on its sword, and brutality. The power of Rome
depended on its army, its ability to conquer and extract wealth
from the conquered territories. The Roman state underwent a
political transformation, from a republican government with
careful checks on individual power, to an imperial regime where
its Caesars had access to unbridled power and sole control over
the might of the armies. Rome was the power of a bullying
nation, with bullying leadership within it.

Society reflected this brutality. Mafia gangs patrolled the
streets and ports and controlled the trade. The ruling elite
engaged in power struggles, with friendship a formal alliance
based on mutual mistrust, Rome a city of filthy tenements, gang
land brawls, underfed citizens and captive slaves, where
bloodshed was rife, and entertainment gladiatorial death, public
executions.

Loyalty and duty were Rome's virtuous pillars; loyalty to
friends, alliances, the legions and ultimately to the emperor
himself, Caesar; with duty to the state of Rome and all that was
required to defend it. A circle of poets was established under the
imperial leadership to affirm the power of the emperor within
this virtuous framework, with the corpus of works that flowed
from this, Latin literature's equivalent of the Jewish scriptures.

Under the patronage of the Emperor Augustus, Virgil the poet
wrote his epic poem the Aeneid, myths surrounding the
foundation of the Roman nation. Where Moses had led the Jews
across the desert to freedom away from the captivity of the
pharaohs in Egypt, Aeneas, the founder of Rome, led the remains
of the defeated Trojan army across the Mediterranean to the

shores of Italy. Both stumbled on their journey.

The Jews worshipped the golden cow, and forgot their faithfulness to God. Aeneas forgot his dutiful purpose to found Rome, falling in love with Dido while ground ashore at Carthage. For Aeneas, duty prevailed as he abandoned his lover, leaving Carthage for the shores of Rome, just as the Jews had regained their faithfulness with victory at Jericho. Along the way, Moses glimpsed God in Heaven as he climbed Sinai to receive the commandments; Aeneas in turn visited his father, and Rome's most glorious dead in the Underworld. Faithfulness led to the survival of the Jews, duty led to the glory of Rome.

Aeneas was dutiful and loyal. He fulfilled his duty to found Rome, and he remained loyal to the memory of his father Anchises. But the corollary was his lack of pity and compassion for the suffering of those who got in the way, and his submission of love to the pursuit of power and glory. Aeneas not only abandoned his lover Dido, who consequently committed suicide, but also left behind his wife and son in Troy. Aeneas did reach Italy, however, and Rome was established.

The spirit of Rome that the story of Aeneas captured, duty over pity, glory over compassion, the Jews were now experiencing first hand. For the cruelty of the Roman procurators sparked the Jewish uprising, with its suppression by the Roman army utter and complete. Jerusalem was levelled to the ground, the remnants of the uprising massacred at Massada.

Rome was brutality and force, God in the New Testament, by contrast, love and compassion, with love the cornerstone of the stories surrounding Jesus. Duty and loyalty were virtues in Rome, but not love and compassion, society too dangerous and brutal to allow them. Compassion was weakness, and led to the compassionate being attacked. Jesus was the opposite, devoted to the poor, the weak, the oppressed, and the most vulnerable elements of society, the beatitudes, a schematic diametrically opposed to the Roman army and its 'brutalitudes'; Jesus the compassionate representative of the poor, the meek, the hungry, the persecuted, the bereaved in the face of Rome's wealth, might, power and sword; Jesus the embracer of the lepers, the outcasts, the downtrodden, the judged and condemned, humanity at all its levels.

The core emotion emanating from Jesus was one of compassionate love, inspired by the brutal assaults on Jewish society and individuals within it by the Romans, a reaction to the cruelty of their actions. The Roman soldiers brutalised Jesus with the scourge, mocked him with the crown of thorns, and slammed the nails into his hands and feet. Crucifixion was the Roman way of killing, extended torture leading to death, with Jesus, the personification of compassion and love, its victim. Jesus was the pacifist in response, with one cheek hit, he offered the other. Jesus rose from the dead, triumphed over the Crucifixion, and survived the Roman brutality. The Christian Jew could lose his body to the Roman, but not his soul, the cross the symbol of defiance over oppression, not through violence, but endurance, knowing that love and compassion could beat brutality and win with the afterlife, the reward, and the victory. The Caesars of Rome were the might, Jesus the compassion to respond.

"Blessed are the peacemakers, for they will be called children of God."
Matthew

6 The Book of Philosophies

Christian spirituality had its roots in Greek philosophy as much as Judaism itself.

The ancient Greeks farmed the land and fished the seas against a backdrop of mountains, cliffs, volcanoes and valleys that inspired them to believe in gods that represented the forces of nature, cycles of life and procreation. Distinct communities evolved with the cities separated by the rough terrain, Sparta a military garrison of severe physical hardship where surrender was disgrace, Athens a naval base, and centre of philosophical thought where citizens had an equal vote.

Democracy took root in fifth century BC Athens, replacing the tyrannies and kings. Trial by jury was established, with the Athenian citizens the jurors appointed daily by random selection. Debates on the nature of justice and wider philosophical issues were commonplace.

Aeschylus' great poetic work, the Oresteia, focused on the evolution from justice by vengeance, blood for blood that could affect a sequence of generations, to justice by jury. Greeks were exploratory in their thinking, rewarding intelligence, with Athena, the goddess of intelligence, the patron of Athens, the owl her emblem.

Like Moses 'the deliverer' and his journey across the desert towards the faithfulness of the tribe, and Aeneas and his voyage across the seas towards his dutiful founding of Rome, Odysseus 'the wayfarer' travelled across the islands, with his wily intelligence the key to finding his way home. The Greeks as a nation finally came of age through their intelligence, just as the Jews had done with their faithfulness, and the Romans with their duty. As it was with wit and foresight that the Greeks finally beat off the Persian invasion in the early 5th century BC craftily abandoning Athens ahead of the advancing Persians, and launching a surprise attack from their nimble ships at Salamis.

Plato and Aristotle each developed concept thinking in their philosophical writings. Aristotle was interested in the nature of man's behaviour, how it was different from animals, and how the structure of society replicated man's nature.

Plato was primarily interested in concept thinking; what was justice, beauty, virtue. He devoted a whole book to love, The Symposium, a dinner party attended by his teacher Socrates, with love discussed in its ascendant forms, from love that was base, and physically driven, to ascetic love that was pure.

Rather than writing his thoughts as a straight thesis, Plato developed his writings as a sequence of dialogues, with Socrates the core protagonist, asking those around him what was justice, what constituted a just action and why, and seeking to lead to his opponents along a path that would lose the argument by self contradiction.

Socrates 'big head' was Plato's teacher and inspiration, with Plato's writings composed after his teacher's death, an extrapolation of his original thinking. Socrates fell foul of the law, his thoughts clearly a threat to the democratic authorities, and was sentenced to death. He had questioned individuals in the democracy to define justice and goodness, given their democratic role as judge and juror, and had found them unable to answer, with lack of critical understanding. Socrates' alternative was a structured society, totalitarian and communist in its make-up. The democratic framework of free speech was unable to withstand such subversive outspokenness. He was imprisoned in a cave just beneath the Parthenon and city forum, where he drunk hemlock and died.

Equipped with the works of Plato and Aristotle, and a host of other philosophical thinkers, the arrival of the Greeks into Jewish territory was as much an ideological threat as it was military. Palestine fell to Greek control under Ptolemy in 301 BC, with the Jews duly forced to pay taxes to the Greeks. Despite being allowed to keep their faith, the strict boundaries of religious adherence were under considerable threat, with the Jews introduced to the more abstract, philosophical and exploratory thinking of the Greeks in comparison to their own intransigent religious law, Judaism scrutinised, probed and undermined.

The Apocrypha was written after the arrival of the Greeks, its style and thoughts influenced by their philosophy, exploring reason over emotions in a story of shocking brutality and courage that closed the Apocryphal writings. A mother had watched six of her seven sons being horribly tortured and executed for refusing to eat meat profane to Jewish custom. The youngest was now encouraged by the tyrant to eat the meat and survive. With his mother imploring him to remain true to his beliefs, they both jumped into the flames, martyrs suffering the agonies of fire.

The writer told the story, and now analysed the behaviour within it, Greek in its philosophical exploration, dwelling on the virtue of the mother's reason over emotion.

"Devout reason is the master of all emotions, not only of those sufferings from within, but also of those from without" Maccabees

7 The Book of Psychologies

The Christian division between body and soul drew on Plato especially.

The Greek philosophers formed the springboard for the more systematic and conceptual thinking of the New Testament writings. Inspired by the bravery and defiance of Daniel, and the death and Resurrection of Jesus, the early Christian Jews were now making a philosophical distinction between an individual's body and its soul. The Roman soldiers could crush Jewish society, and break individuals within it, but the soul could survive, independent of what happened to the body.

Plato had separated human psychology into three components – reason, courage and desire. Jewish Christian thinking was simpler, with the twofold division of body and soul, or flesh and will. The flesh represented the sin, whereas the will was now the internal power of the soul required to prevent the body from yielding to sin. The body operated in the physical world with its physical urges, the soul in the spiritual world, with the Christian drawing on the 'Holy Spirit' to give it discipline.

Such systematic philosophical thinking formed the foundations of Paul's writings in his New Testament letters. He promoted living in the spirit, rather than living in the flesh, begrudgingly accepting the necessity of physical love, and would rather cut off his right arm than suffer male temptation.

What started off as Daniel keeping true to his God, despite the threats of death, and the seven sons enduring terrible tortures but not eating the meat, ended with Jesus being nailed to the cross in agonising pain so his soul could resurrect and transform into a wider application of living. The flesh was human, therefore capable of sin; the soul was divine, and capable of salvation. Abstain from physical pleasure, as the enjoyment of the flesh pertained to sin. Have sex if you must, but remain sober. As it was the soul that was more important, with the hope of immortality in Heaven, provided the body abstained.

Philo, the Jewish philosopher, 20 BC to AD 50, was contemporary to the life of Jesus, and the early Jewish Christian movement. Philo in his works drew strongly on the Greek philosophers for the drivers and explanations of human behaviour, not least Plato's three fold psychology of reason, courage and desire. From this he developed his own schematic, with man driven by earthiness or sensibility, but also by spirituality or reason. Without the body and sex man could be morally perfect, but the body was a source of danger, and one that could drag the spirit into the bonds of sensibility.

Christianity seized on the sensibility and spirituality split, and translated it into the dichotomy of the body and soul, thereby submitting the body and its earthy desires to the soul and its Heavenly afterlife.

Philo saw 'logos', the Greek for word or explanation, as God's creative principle. John's New Testament gospel, and his narrative of the life of Jesus, was cloaked in such language, opening with his thesis, that the word and God were one and the same, with the word becoming flesh. The tone was set for a gospel that explored the concept of love, equating it to life and God himself, and, although not explicit, offering an answer to Socrates' exploration of love in Plato's symposium. God was love, and Jesus the human embodiment of that love.

This impact of Greek philosophical thinking was, of course, not just limited to the Jews but influential across the wider Mediterranean world. Rome may well have conquered Greece, but it was the Greek ideals that had conquered Rome.

Groups and sects of philosophers were widespread and various, the Epicureans, the Stoics, the Cynics, and among them were now the Christians, a new philosophical sect, challenging not only the thinking of other philosophical groups, but the foundations of Judaism itself. The early Christian thinkers had merged Plato with Judaism, with Christianity evolving in its wake.

"And the Word became flesh and lived among us." John

8 The Book of Scribes

The gospel construction of the life of Jesus drew as much on the Socratic dialogues of Plato as the Old Testament for its basic framework and presentation of thought.

Coincident to the First Jewish war in Jerusalem, a contingent of Christians gathered 300 miles north in Antioch to compile their new spiritual thesis. Their task was daunting yet simple, to relate the life of Jesus, the new super hero of salvation, in a way that captured the core elements of their new sect. The group had studied Greek philosophy and the Jewish scriptures, the format and content of their narratives to form a synthesis of the two.

First and foremost were the echoes of Old Testament stories

embedded within the gospel framework, with the life of Jesus narrated as a micro version of the history of Judaism. Jesus spent his early years in exile in Egypt, where the Jews centuries before had been held captive. Moses and the tribes wandered the desert for 40 years, suffering the temptations of idolatry, with their faith tested on the way. Jesus entered the desert for 40 days and 40 nights with his faith tested by Satan. Moses fed the tribe crossing the desert with manna and quails from heaven; Jesus fed the 5000 with loaves and fish.

The 12 tribes entered the promised land of Canaan, with Joshua leading his army in triumph and the Jewish state to salvation. Jesus in turn led his 12 disciples to a message of personal salvation through triumph over sin. Jerusalem was conquered with the Jews longing for their homeland in Exile. Jesus was crucified, with his followers bereft of their leader, mourning his death. The prophets looked forward to the return of a new David, and a New Jerusalem. Jesus' followers looked forward to his second coming, and a new Heaven on earth following his Resurrection from the dead.

Plato and his narrations on Socrates provided much of the additional framework. Socrates, whose father was a stonemason, walked among the democratic community of Athens and challenged its thinking. Jesus, whose father was a carpenter, walked among the Jewish community in Galilee and challenged its spiritual leadership in Jerusalem. Socrates was sentenced to death on grounds of religious and moral subversion, maintaining his spirit of defiance throughout his trial. Jesus was sentenced to death for religious subversion, claiming to be the Son of God, remaining silently defiant during his trial. Each could have saved himself from execution, Socrates by suggesting an alternative punishment of banishment, Jesus by performing a miracle; both chose not to. Socrates was imprisoned in a cave outside the main city centre, where he drunk hemlock, and suffered its slow and painful death. Jesus was led outside of Jerusalem where he was nailed to a cross and suffered the prolonged horrors of Crucifixion.

Plato had recorded Socrates' thoughts through a sequence of dialogues with people he encountered in the company of his friends in Athens. A premise was raised or a question asked, and a conclusion drawn from the interchange that followed, the dialectic process. The core content of the gospel was written in much the same way to represent the conversations and engagements Jesus had with his friends, his disciples, and people he encountered on his wanderings, frequently recorded in Plato's dialectic style.

Plato included a number of parables told by Socrates in his stories, to make a point, and to shed greater light on the thoughts of Socrates. The use of parables to facilitate teaching, and add clarity to a point was, of course, universal, and steeped in Jewish as well as Greek tradition. Such parables formed the essence of Jesus' communication in the New Testament Gospels, The Prodigal Son, the Good Samaritan, among the many.

One of Plato's parables neatly foretold the life of Socrates in a way that could so easily have been referring to Jesus.

Socrates likened human understanding of reality to men in caves watching shadows of cut outs of real life articles. When one of the group watching left the cave, saw the real articles in daylight and the sun that formed the shadows, and then returned to the cave to tell his cave mates, they killed him, preferring the shadows of cut-outs of reality. Socrates and Jesus each in their own way expounded a higher level of truth to the communities in which they lived, but both paid the price with their lives.

A framework gospel was initially compiled forming a narrative base for the gospels that followed. Matthew, Mark, Luke and John, some of the earliest of the gospel writers, were therefore able to provide a more or less consistent construction of the life of Jesus within a set of boundaries with scope for personal interpretation and artistic license.

In the two centuries that followed many other gospels were written, under the names of individuals, Thomas, Mary Magdelene, Peter, Judas, Philip; and tribes, the Hebrews, the Egyptians, the Ebionites, the Nazoreans; and virtues, Truth.

These later gospels were more theoretical and specific in content, with limited if any reference to physical places, or historical settings, the gospel of Judas exploring Judas' role as Jesus' betrayer as an example. The four gospels that were eventually chosen for the New Testament admirably achieved their purpose though, portraying the life of Jesus in line with the new spiritual system of Christianity.

"I too decided, after investigating everything very carefully from the very first, to write an orderly account for you" Luke

9 The Book of Locations

To construct the detail of Jesus' life, the gospel writers drew on a range of traditional settings and techniques, with events prophesised in the Jewish scriptures and the miracles that Jesus performed essential to the narrative.

Luke claimed in the opening of his gospel to be relying on the written accounts of eye witnesses, a literary device in the tradition of the Greek historians Herodotus and Xenophon to give authority to his work. For the New Testament Gospels were composed 30 or so years after Jesus' timeline, and several hundred miles away from where the recorded events were based. The chance of anyone living in Antioch in AD 65 who had lived at Capernaum on Lake Galilee hundreds of miles away some 35 years before was exponentially remote.

The geographical settings of Jesus' ministry were relatively straightforward to achieve. Jerusalem, Nazareth, and the Sea of Galilee were either known personally or second hand to the gospel writers. The recent exodus from Jerusalem and the surrounding areas, to north Syria where the New Testament Gospels were being compiled included people from all of these locations.

The inclusion of recent events and characters into the gospel stories lent colour, but more importantly validity to the narrative. King Herod was a notorious tyrant who killed his wife and three of his children, with Herod, according to Matthew, giving his order to kill all the babies in Nazareth, and later beheading John the Baptist to please his daughter. Luke integrated the census of Caesar Augustus into his narrative, not that a Jewish carpenter or his wife have actually been required to participate in any such census as they were not citizens.

The birth of a king, most certainly the Jewish Messiah, merited an astronomical event. Persia was renowned for astrologers, or magi, experts of the day in the paths of stars and planets, monitoring for unusual astronomical events that might herald a new event. Coins minted in Antioch from the late first century AD, coincident to the publication of the gospel story of the Star of Bethlehem and the magi's visit to worship the new born king, depicted a star adjacent to a lamb, the star the representation of the birth of the king, the lamb the Jew. The visit of the wise men was an essential component to the narrative construction of Jesus' birth, linking his arrival to movement in the Heavens.

The shepherds in the nativity fields reflected yet another tradition, the birth of new cultures with shepherds in attendance. Coins from ancient Rome depicting Romulus and Remus, the founders of Rome, not only pictured the wolf that suckled them, but shepherds alongside. If Jesus' birth merited movement in the Heavens it also deserved shepherds in attendance, to signify the birth of God's new nation on earth.

Events in Jesus' life, in Matthew's gospel especially, drew on a collection of Old Testament prophecies. The prophets frequently looked forward to a new King David, a restorer of the Jewish nation to its former glories.

The prophecy of Isaiah was in reality nothing more than a typical looking forward of the Jewish nation to a new commander who could reinstate Israel's former greatness over her enemy states. Matthew used it instead as a prediction of Jesus' birth and his later role as saviour of mankind. Jesus' virgin birth in Bethlehem, escape to Egypt, and later return to Nazareth together fulfilled four separate prophecies related to the birth of the new Messianic David. The story of Jesus and his parents fleeing from Bethlehem to Egypt to escape Herod the baby slayer brought together two conflicting Old Testament prophecies in the process, one that the Messiah was to come from Bethlehem, another from Egypt.

John continued Matthew's prophetic pattern in his gospel with his narration of Jesus' Crucifixion; Jesus' drink of vinegar on the cross, the piercing of his body, and lack of broken bones, all matched the predictions of the Old Testament prophets.

Within this historical and prophetic framework, Jesus performed his miracles.

The miracles were allegorical, all made for a point. Jesus' first miracle of turning water into wine was symbolic of the new spirituality being created from an old religious system, with his feeding of the 5000 connecting him back to Moses and the miraculous feeding of the tribe in the desert. In terms of the new spirituality Jesus healing the sick was symbolic of his ability to cleanse the soul, with his raising the dead back to the living, a sign of the promise of afterlife.

Beyond the allegorical content, however, the miracles were as essential as the historical setting itself for the gospels to gain credence with their readers. In a world where people rarely travelled beyond their own established territory, and where proof of what happened miles away was solely reliant on the 'witnesses' who were there, whereby anecdotal stories could soon pass as fact, the fast and fanciful was easily believed. Herodotus the first Greek historian had set the trend with his fantastic accounts of events, with historians that followed copying his style.

Given the tradition of gods and goddesses in Greek mythology shaking Heaven and Earth, God of the Old Testament performing his own miraculous works on behalf of the Jewish tribe, and David the original Messiah slaying a giant with a sling, Jesus' ability to perform miracles was essential for contemporary society to be able to take the new Christian movement seriously.

"But you, O Bethlehem, from you shall come forth from me one who is to rule Israel." Isaiah

10 The Book of Blogs

The New Testament letters pre-dated the gospel constructions, and were published as blogs on the new Christian faith.

The letters followed the four Gospels according to the order of the New Testament, logical in terms of time sequence with the letters forming part of the evangelist outreach of the early Christian movement following the life, death and Resurrection of Jesus. The link between the two was the book of Acts, a narrative of the early evangelical missions of Peter and Paul, an account of the period of their lives when the letters were written by them. But in terms of writing order, the opposite was true, the letters apparently written first AD 50-60, with the four Gospels composed sometime afterwards AD 65-100. Acts was written around AD 80, to link the message of the gospels and the contents of the letters with the wanderings of their authors, as they spread the gospel words across the Mediterranean.

Prior to the composition of the gospel narratives of Jesus, a sequence of letters had already been written to outline the framework of the new spiritual system represented by Christianity. According to these, Jesus was recognised simply as the human embodiment of these new spiritual values, more often than not referred to as Christ rather than Jesus, with Christ a Greek word, literally meaning the anointed one, the Messiah, the one chosen by God, heralding back to David the victorious king of the Jews. Christ in the context of these letters was synonymous with compassion and love, representing both a pacifist acceptance of Roman control, and a critique of the Jewish law. Christ's Crucifixion was the consequence to such political and religious stance, with his Resurrection the answer. Christ's Last Supper, as outlined in these letters, with the symbols of bread and wine for sacrifice, was core to this new spiritualised system.

The letter attributed to James was the earliest, composed around AD 50. No mention was made of Jesus at all in its meanderings on faith and works, and support for the Jewish law. This reflected the timing of the letter when Christianity was still evolutionary, where the life of Jesus was not yet essential to the message contained, and where the sect was still firmly embedded in Judaism.

The letters essentially formed a sequence of blogs on the new Christian movement. Although formally addressed, whether to a nation, the Romans, or an individual, Timothy, they were designed for wide scale general distribution, addressing specific issues 'pertinent' to the named recipient, but applicable to all those who read them. Certain themes pervaded: the role of the Holy Spirit, the struggle between the physical urges of the body and the spiritual aspirations of the soul, the promise of salvation and new life, the expected behaviour of the church, and acceptance of political structures. Each letter also had a specific point, however, underlined by the chosen recipient.

The message that Christianity was not subversive to political structures, rather accepting of them as God's will, was contained within a letter formally addressed to the leadership of the day, the Romans. The message was equally applicable to all those who wished to follow the new faith, the need to yield to the authority of kings and government. Society's laws were to be kept as part of God's divination, regardless of the spirituality of the individual. The Corinthians were the named recipients of a letter regarding sexual immorality, and the need to give to the poor; homosexuality was mainstream to Greek society, with Corinth no exception, and of the Greek cities, notably elitist. But the message was applicable to all followers of the new egalitarian sect, with sexual morality a pre-requisite in the struggle between body and soul.

Each letter had a focus that somehow reflected the named recipient; Philippines, the need for humility, given its special status as a Roman colony; Colossians, the avoidance of philosophy and magic, given the renown of Colossus as a centre of mysticism; Ephesians, the need for fellowship across the entire Christian community, Ephesus a cosmopolitan port, a city of nightlife.

The letter to the Hebrews was effectively an address to the Jews, exploring stories of faithfulness in the Old Testament as examples for faithfulness to Jesus; the old religious system had been supplanted by a new spirituality with Jesus greater than Moses. Hebrews was a letter of encouragement to the Jews to move on, and redirect their faith of Abraham towards Jesus.

Alongside the epistles addressed to groups were letters to individuals, meant for a wider audience, not just the named recipient, letters to Timothy, and Titus dealing with the wider issues of the social fabric of Christian gatherings in terms of pastoral care and leadership.

The Christian church was to be elder based, reflecting the

patriarchy of the day, with overseers and mediators on points of discussion, but in a flat structured hierarchy where all were equal in the eyes of God.

The letter to Philemon dealt with the role and treatment of slaves. The author of the letter was intervening on behalf of the slave Onesimus, 'Useful', given the grievances he had against his master, Philemon, 'Love-myself'. Onesimus was now a brother in Christ; he may well be a slave in society, but from God's vantage he was 'free'.

The message affirmed that Christianity was not meant to be subversive to existing structures in society. Slavery was acceptable. As was male dominance, a message set out in a further letter to Timothy, with the male the master of the house, the woman to learn in silence with full submission; God created Adam before Eve, with Eve being the first to be deceived by the serpent in the garden.

"I permit no woman to teach or to have authority over a man; she is to keep silent." Timothy

11 The Book of Letters

Authorship of these letters was attributed to characters associated with Jesus, along with the evangelist Paul the main character in the later narratives of Acts.

The letters were attributed to five individuals, Paul, Peter, James, Jude and John. They had been written by the early Christian movement, with pseudonyms used to enhance their credibility, James the brother of Jesus, and Peter his disciple. With such authorship, the letter writers were granted ultimate authority with first-hand knowledge of Jesus.

The majority of the letters were attributed to Paul, with the opening of his letter to the Galatians his autobiography and CV, his credentials as Christian letter writer. In it Paul admitted to being a former persecutor of the Christians, claiming to have received God's message on Jesus and salvation directly from God himself. His mission was to introduce Jesus to the Gentiles, with the credentials of personally knowing some of the disciples personally, Peter, James and John. In fact he had already been on the missionary road for at least 18 years, in his specific mission to reach out to the Gentiles. Paul had the perfect CV for a Christian sermon writer, with the model conversion from Judaism to Christian, from persecutor to missionary, equipped with a message given directly from God. His conversion was a paradigm of all conversions to come, open to Gentiles, even Christian persecutors.

Some of his letters appeared to be written from a prison cell, with persecution part of the expected Christian framework. Although the early Christian movement was essentially pacifist, it challenged Judaism with its new spirituality and Rome with its failure to recognise the Roman gods, and the emperor as its divine leader. Jesus was tried by the Jews, the religious system, and crucified by the Romans, the political body, with Paul, according to Luke's narrative of Acts, convicted by the Jews, travelling to Rome for trial.

Devices of authorship, life credentials, and dramatic settings all combined to support the authority of the writers. The letter wrapper was its seal, with each sermon personally addressed, a recognised literary device, and a way of publishing a tract or thesis to a wider audience beyond the stated recipient.

The letters of Paul varied in their personal content. Some had the briefest of pre-ambles written in a formalised style 'Paul, to the saints who are in Ephesus'.

Others were considerably more personalised, with the letters to Timothy stating a wish to see his friend again, and information and instructions on people and friends they knew and shared in common. But even in these more personalised letters the friendly pre-amble quickly reverted to a sermon or thesis, with the friend to whom the letter was addressed losing any personal connection.

"To Timothy, my loyal child in the faith" Timothy

12 *The Book of Humilities*

Paul formed the perfect conversion, with his evangelism and voyage to Rome an allegory of the new wave of Christianity spreading through the Jewish synagogues across the Mediterranean world.

In AD 80 Luke wrote his narrative of the first apostles, Peter and Paul, the letter writers, in his book Acts. The first few chapters were devoted to Peter, 'the rock', with Paul, 'the humble', the lead in the second half. Both had equally important roles: Peter, as Jesus' disciple, connected the early missionary work of the Christians to Jesus himself; Paul was crucial in extending the message beyond the Jews to the Gentiles, essentially the Greeks. Peter as the 'rock' was the foundation of the message, and Paul its 'humble' expounder to the world.

Paul was a human embodiment of Christian conversion, and evangelism, just as Jesus was the human embodiment of God's salvation, and Daniel of defiance under imperial oppression. Saul on conversion was renamed Paul. Back in 1000 BC his namesake King Saul had been consumed by jealousy for David, the slayer of Goliath, and had committed suicide following his failed attempts to kill him. Saul was a failed military leader, and Messianic assassin. Saul in Luke's narration of Acts was a Roman citizen but also a persecutor of those following the new Christian faith in his role as a Pharisee. Like his namesake Saul was working against the Messianic force of Jesus the new David. He was neatly representative of the two forces that early Christianity was challenging, the Jewish law, and the military might of Rome.

On Saul's conversion to Christianity he was renamed Paul through one change of letter, in one stroke adopting Gentile status, Paul a Greek name, transforming from Saul, the Messianic assassin, to Paul an embodiment of the Christian spiritual values of compassion for the oppressed and humility, Paul in Greek meaning 'small, humble'. Saul became Paul, discarding the Jewish name and mantle of Roman citizenship, adopting instead the inner spirituality of the humble Christian in the face of imperial might and intransigence of the Jewish Law. Saul was symbolic of the Roman and Jewish constraints to freedom, Paul of the new internal freedom offered by the Christian Jews as a Covenant to the rest of the world.

Equipped with the various letters of Paul written 20 to 30 years earlier, not least his CV in Galatians, Luke compiled his narrative of Paul's life as a missionary, an allegory of the spread of the new Christian movement across the Mediterranean. To gain readership, Luke's narrations of the lives of the early missionaries in Acts were dramatically portrayed and memorable in vision. In the opening chapters Jesus ascended to Heaven with two men in robes standing by him, with tongues of fire descending upon each of the apostles. Blessed with the Holy Spirit the apostles drove out demons and performed miracles.

In contrast, Ananias and his wife were struck down dead, and Herod died eaten by worms. Paul was struck blind by a vision from Heaven, scales falling from his eyes so he could see; he later survived four storms, a deadly snake, a shipwreck, and earthquake in prison. The Gentile audiences would have listened spell bound and believed!

Acts was not, as Luke would have wished the reader to believe, a factual account of what actually happened to Saul turned Paul, the small and humble, single-handedly founding the churches from Syria to Greece across to Rome itself.

The reality was more mundane and simple, the new wave of Christian thinking gradually spreading through the Jewish synagogues by general word of mouth, across the various pockets of the Roman Empire, an evolutionary thought, not because of Paul or any other individual traversing the Mediterranean to deliver the message.

Acts in this regard was typical of the New Testament style, fanciful and vivid as it sought to capture the core message of the new Christian movement, with Luke's gospel writings and his narration of Acts over the centuries that followed successfully acquainting the world with a spiritual system based on love, compassion, and physical abstinence, with an afterlife in Heaven. The New Testament combination of gospels and letters proved marketing genius, with Jesus at the centre, the collective passion and voice of the early Christians as they disengaged from the external trappings of Judaism against a backdrop of Roman persecution.

"And immediately, because Herod had not given the glory to God, an angel of the Lord struck him down, and he was eaten by worms and died." Acts

The Revelation of Challenges

The combination of gospels and letters formed a message of hope and love to the tribes and nations oppressed by the imperial force of Rome, a spiritualised version of Judaism, embroidered in Greek philosophy, with the promise of after-life regardless of race.

The spiritual system of early Christianity had evolved over time and as a response to a sequence of imperial incursions. The Christian sect of the Jews had formulated a message that they now felt confident to share.

God had already demonstrated his faithfulness to protect and also his power to punish via his special pact with the Jews. Now God turned his attention to non Jews as well. The enemy was no longer non Jewish, but anyone who failed to recognise God as their saviour. Salvation was no longer the survival of the Jewish tribe against their enemies, but of the individual against sin, with an after-life in Heaven.

The construct of the New Testament scriptures portrayed the emergence of this new faith as a straight sequence of actual events, the narrative of the life, death and Resurrection of Jesus, followed by the evangelism of the message by Peter and Paul.

God sent his Son Jesus to Earth. Although the Son of God, Jesus' human background was humble, born in a stable in Bethlehem, and brought up in rural Galilee by Joseph a carpenter. As an adult he led his life as a human demonstration of God's love in the midst of the Jews, who still believed that God favoured them above all others, and the Romans, the political force of suppression at the time. He chose a small group of disciples, and taught them about God's love, his compassion, and his ability to heal, and most of all about his forgiveness of their sins, with the promise of eternal life.

After preaching to the crowds in Galilee, he travelled to

Jerusalem, where he criticised the Pharisees for treating the Temple as a trading place rather than a hallowed place of worship. The Jews convicted Jesus for heresy, given his claim that he was the Son of God, and the Romans carried out the Crucifixion. But Jesus rose from the dead on the third day after his execution, conqueror over these evil forces.

God triumphed over sin and death and his pact passed from the Jews to all those who believed in him. Man from this moment on had a choice, to believe in God, Jesus and love, or to follow the world of sin and miss out on eternity with God in Heaven. Jesus went back to Heaven a few days after his Resurrection, but not before he had commanded his disciples to spread his message of love and forgiveness to all mankind.

Christians, Peter and Paul initially, evangelised the news of God's love via Jesus, and the message of the New Testament, with the message spreading beyond the racial limitations of the Jews to the Gentiles, even to Rome.

All who received this message were in a position of choice, to choose God and salvation, and be cleansed from their sin, or ignore him, remain in sin, and suffer eternity without him, in Hell.

The Christian narrative had been formed, and now like many emerging faiths of the time, those who heard it could accept it or reject it, become Christians, and face martyrdom and Heaven thereafter, or remain entrenched in a physical society controlled by the Roman sword.

The Jews could retain their religious practices in their foreign enclaves, the Greeks could pursue their philosophies and pleasures, the Romans could continue to suppress. Or the teachings of Jesus could be followed, a spiritual life of physical abstinence regardless of political control, with an afterlife with God in Heaven.

"'Go therefore and make disciples of all nations'" Matthew

Testament 111 The State

The uses of the Christian faith by the politicians in their attempts to install religious conformity and social control

The books

1	Persecutions	5	Devils	9	Crusaders
2	Gentiles	6	Politics	10	Confessions
3	Triumphs	7	Popes	11	Monarchs
4	Romans	8	Arabs	12	Divisions
Revelation	Spires				

Roman persecution of the Christians under the Emperor Nero inspired the writings of Revelation.

The persecutions stopped when Rome converted to Christianity some 300 years later. Various strands of Christianity, Roman paganism and Judaism were gathered together into a new universal brand of state religion, Catholicism, forged to suit the imperial establishment.

Subjects were easier to control if they believed they were sinners aspiring to an afterlife, with the Devil and Hell exploited as instruments of state control. Christianity was less about spiritual freedom more about political control, with flames of agony for the dissenters.

The pope and Roman Church took up the religious reins from the collapsed imperial system, followed by national monarchs as countries gained political power.

The Bible and its texts were interpreted according to the political needs of those in power and the social and moral agenda of the day, with execution for those who disagreed.

The divinity of monarchs eventually gave way to a wider upper class and a greater role for government. The Bible continued to be used as a weapon of social control, despite these changes, with the powerfully symbolic connection between religion and monarchy surviving.

1 The Book of Persecutions

Revelation captured the battle for the soul between the Christians and the politicians, with Nero's persecution of Christianity setting the pace.

In AD 64 Christians in Rome were rounded up, bound to stakes and burnt alive in their dozens while the glutinous Nero dined in an open courtyard nearby listening to their shrieks like music. This was their punishment for the fire of Rome that weeks before had destroyed swathes of the city, blamed for their failure to recognise the Roman gods and goddesses, and worse still to acknowledge Nero as an emperor with divine status.

The image of Christianity as a persecuted faith had been powerfully captured by the New Testament writings. Jesus was tried by the Jews, and crucified by the Romans. According to the later narrative of Acts Stephen was the first martyr, stoned to death by the Jews, in the presence of Saul, a Pharisee and Roman Citizen. Paul, according to the same narration, was later condemned by the Jews, travelling to Rome as its citizen to appeal to the Emperor.

There was much about Christianity to invite such persecution. Mainstream Jews reacted negatively to the Christians; not only had they robbed them of their own Messianic expectation through Jesus, they had also undermined their racial purity by embracing the Gentiles. The religious industry of pagan worship was also under threat. Visits to the pagan sites at Ephesus, the epicentre of the new Christian faith, were profitable business, and vulnerable to new and growing sects. Unlike Judaism, where race barred entry, Christianity was advertised as open to all. Above all Christian refusal to acknowledge the emperor as divine unsettled the Roman authorities. Romans were suspicious of unauthorised sects and group meetings, the Christians no exception, regarded as cannibals, eating the human flesh and drinking the blood of Jesus.

As an answer to specific acts of Roman persecution, in AD 95 John wrote Revelation. His writings were part of an apocalyptic tradition, subversive and in code that imagined the destruction of an evil world and its heavenly replacement. This literary device stemmed from the Jews post Exile, with the book of Daniel writing on the fall of Babylon, as a guise for the hoped for collapse of Syrian oppression. The Christians quickly adopted apocalyptic writing as their own.

On this occasion John's subversive energy was directed at Rome the great dragon, the ancient serpent, 666, Nero himself, the deceiver with authority over every tribe, people, and nation. The dragon had drunk the blood of its saints and witnesses of Jesus. Babylon, coded for Rome, would therefore collapse under the seven bowls of wrath, the sores, the death of the seas, the rivers turned to blood, sun scorching the earth, the ensuing darkness, the foul spirits emerging from the Euphrates, and the earthquake from Babylon. In its place the Son of Man was set to come, sickle in hand, gathering the vintage of the earth, the Christians, the great wine press, God the victor over Satan, symbolically Rome no more.

The engagement between Christianity and politics had begun, with Nero's burning of the Christians on the site that would eventually become the seat of Christendom itself, the Vatican. The early Christian focus was on the soul outside of political influence, Jesus teaching obedience to the political system, Give to Caesar what is Caesar's, and Paul in his letter to the Romans, claiming all political systems to be God ordained and thereby obeyed. But the mission of the politicians now extended to the soul itself, a mission that would last for the ages to come.

What their subjects believed on the inside was now as important as their outer obedience to any political or military rule. If the emperor Nero believed he was divine, it was essential that all his subjects actively shared this belief that he was a god, even unto death. The stage was set for the battle between the individual and the politicians, the freedom of internal belief, soul and speech, the submersion of the soul by the politician.

"Fallen, fallen is Babylon the great! She has made all nations drink of the wine of the wrath of her fornication" Revelation

2 The Book of Gentiles

Christianity's early popularity reflected an Empire seeking spiritual refuge from the physical oppression of its army and leaders.

By the end of the third century AD, early Christianity had spread across the Roman Empire, in the face of pagan traditions and political suppression. Whether by accident or design Christianity had been programmed for success by its Jewish architects.

What had started as a way of sustaining Jewish ideology through its spiritual internalisation was fast becoming Christian-mania seeping the four quadrants of the Roman imperial world.

Key to its success was its racial openness. The last book of the Old Testament, Malachi, reiterated the rule that Jews should not marry outside their race. But when Jesus the Jew was asked in the

New Testament who was his neighbour he told the story of the Good Samaritan. The Samaritans were mixed race, Jewish and Gentile, despised by the Jews for what they represented, members of their community marrying or having children outside of their racial boundaries.

The love of Jesus, however, now embraced the Samaritan with his message of empathy regardless of race. God was no longer the god of one tribe to the exclusion of others, but of all mankind. The Covenant with the Jews according to Christian thinking had been replaced by a wider Covenant with humanity in general.

The foundations for Jewish and Gentile cohesion had been set over the 300 years preceding the Good Samaritan, with mutual respect and cultural bonding developing between elements of the Jewish and Greeks communities.

Roman oppression proved the catalyst towards a more radical integration, a move from Jewish exclusivity to wider cultural tolerance. Issues of race and health that had previously barred entrance to the Jewish Temple were barriers no more to this new spirituality. Christianity evolved from Greek philosophy and Jewish religion, with Greeks and Jews alike suffering under the control of Rome's military might.

For the first time in Jewish history, Jews and non Jews had a clear common enemy, the Romans. The entire region was engulfed by Roman oppression, with the earlier enemies of the Jews, the Syrians, Greeks and Egyptians all united in their subjugation to Rome and the Caesars. If the various nations no longer had the power to unite and fight back with physical weaponry, a united front could at least be offered in the spiritual sphere, the Romans behind their military standards, the Christians behind the crucifix of physical oppression, their symbol of hope and love.

The initial response of pacifism of the new sect of Christians stood in comparison to the main stream Jews who responded with violent resistance to the powers of Rome and were crushed together with their Temple as a consequence.

Beyond the oppressive presence of the Romans, wider more fundamental shifts were also sweeping the Mediterranean world, with societies moving on from their belief in pagan gods. The exploratory thinking of the Greek philosophers, mathematicians and scientists were taking the psychology of the Mediterranean world beyond the pagan rites and devotions to their panoply of Gods. Greeks and Romans alike were questioning their superstitions and beliefs in Zeus and Jupiter, Aphrodite and Venus, Artemis and Ceres. A spiritual gap was emerging, with Christianity the candidate to fill it, Greek philosophical systems at its core, Plato and Socrates at its base, and all races able to participate.

"But a Samaritan bandaged his wounds and took care of him" Luke

3 The Book of Triumphs

Constantine's super plan was to reunite the Roman Empire and become sole emperor, with his conversion to Christianity a critical step towards this goal.

Despite its expansion, the Christian movement met quietly in homes, secretly in caves and catacombs, to avoid detection and persecution. But with the trend of expansion accelerating, towards the end of the third century AD the Emperor Diocletian ordered the destruction of any places of Christian worship, and the execution of the Christians themselves.

The tipping point of Christian popularity versus pagan tradition had been reached.

Martyrdom was the Christian response, cheek with cheek pacifists in the tradition of Stephen, and Jesus himself. Herded into the theatres across the Empire, the Coliseum at Rome, slaughtered for sport, fed to the lions, burnt alive, they responded with bravery and calm, and like superstar gladiators, won over the crowds. Most disconcertingly for the imperial regime, the appeal of Christianity was permeating the ranks of aristocrats. Even Helena, the mother of the Emperor Constantine, Diocletian's successor, converted to the faith, travelling to Jerusalem on a pilgrimage.

Amid all of this was Constantine, a shrewd politician, hugely ambitious, and a smart military tactician, who, 18 years into his reign in AD 324, secured the merger of the eastern and western halves of the Roman Empire. He abolished the system of four co-emperors and achieved his goal, the sole emperorship of a unified Empire.

Constantine's first task to achieve this ambition was to oust Maxentius his western co-emperor. On the eve of the crucial battle at Milvian Bridge in AD 306, Constantine converted to Christianity, claiming to have received visions from God the night before. The next day he won the battle, the enemy in disarray, confused by his military standards, and soldier uniforms now bearing the Christian cross. Like Saul becoming Paul, Constantine saw a vision, with conversion leading to his evangelism for the Empire.

Underneath the guise of a miraculous conversion, shrewd and long term tactics were at play. Constantine recognised the growth trend in the Christian movement, in the East especially. If he lost to Maxentius, he would die, regardless of his conversion. But if he won under the Christian banner, his adoption of Christianity would be vindicated, and he would be seen with the Christian God on his side. This he affirmed by holding a triumph in Rome to celebrate the victory; the de-capitated head of his defeated opponent Maxentius, retrieved from the Tiber, was brandished on high, with Christianity paraded through the streets and forum of Rome a triumphant religion, Constantine its core sponsor.

In AD 324 Constantine became sole emperor of a unified Christian realm defeating Lucinius his imperial counterpart in the east. The cost to the precepts on which early Christianity had been founded were huge, with the individual spirituality for which countless Christian martyrs had died lost to Christianity's new role as state religion.

The Jewish Temple that had been made redundant to Christians by the spiritual temple inside the body was now usurped by basilica buildings of worship. The priests that had been made unnecessary by an internalised relationship with God were replenished by a new and reinvigorated priesthood of Christians.

For in pomp, superstition and ceremony Christianity reverted to the state religion of Judaism but on a far grander scale, not just for the Jews, but for all who lived in the Roman Empire, the four corners of Christendom.

"Hallelujah! For the lord our God omnipotent reigns" Revelation

4 The Book of Romans

Core elements of Judaism, Christianity and Roman paganism were merged into one, to form the new state religion, Roman Catholicism.

Ostensibly, Christianity was the core beneficiary of Constantine's revision of the Roman religious system, with the pagan tradition-alists the losers. The reality was somewhat different with Constantine showering the traditional Roman priesthood with wealth and power to compensate. Pagan priests in Rome and across the Empire had traditionally managed the religious fabric. More importantly they performed sacrifices, and consulted the omens to determine military or political strategy. Their say over the political elite was real and tangible, with the role of high priest, the pontifex maximus, a key step in the political ladder of the Roman Republic towards becoming consul, leader of the senate. Julius Caesar held the role before becoming consul, and effective dictator. With the formal residence of the high priest located in the centre of the Roman forum, the heart of political life, the post commanded maximum respect.

With the advent of Christianity, the priesthood needed a replacement role, achieved by cloning the Roman religious structure onto the Christian spiritual system.

In Rome the panoply of gods communicated to the people via the priest. From now on, according to the Roman interpretation of Christianity, communication from God to the people would also be via the priest, with the Roman high priest now the ultimate voice of authority on God's will. At the local level the priest listened to the confessions of the individual Christians, and determined an appropriate response, or prayer for the sin committed. Forgiveness for sins was no longer directly from God via Jesus, but dependent on the priest.

By far the most important elevation of the priesthood, however, was his role at the ceremony of Holy Communion, the celebration of the Last Supper. Given that the Roman Church from the outset had ordained that the bread and wine were literally the body and blood of Jesus via transubstantiation, it was for the priest only to administer God's blood for the worshippers. The priest thereby retained his sacrificial role, with the divine blood of Jesus replacing the blood of a slain animal.

Roman religion and the 'pagan' people of Rome also needed compensation. To achieve this Constantine installed religious building works of munificence under the umbrella of the new Christian faith, with the church granted tax exempt status.

The first place of formal worship for the Christians in Rome had initially been designated as the forum's basilica, the trading place, and market. Larger considerably more substantial basilicas were soon to be built on the peripheries of the city, located away from the traditional Roman Temples centred round the forum to underline the religious break with the old system.

The structure of these new 'churches' were based on the framework of the initial basilica, a nave and wings or transepts either side, with an apse at the end. The rich adornments of these buildings were beyond compare, with gold, marble, statues, frescoes, art and carved stone. Christian building works across the Empire were also initiated, not least in Jerusalem itself with the pagan city of Hadrian rebuilt with beautiful basilicas not around the Jewish centres where the Temple had once stood, but areas where Jesus had suffered.

Rome itself was suddenly promoted as the centre of this new Christian religion. Folklore had already established the Crucifixion of Peter as part of Nero's revenge, with Paul beheaded by a Roman sword for failing to renounce his faith. The letter of Paul to the Romans, and Luke's account of Paul's voyage to Rome in Acts affirmed this connection. Paul's letter to the Romans was of particular interest to Constantine, as it affirmed that all political structures were God ordained; it was therefore God's will for Constantine to be sole emperor of the Roman Empire, the new Christendom. Peter's role as the stone, the foundation of the Christian church, was literally to be cemented in Rome, affirmed by the basilica built in his memory with his tomb beneath its foundation on the site where Nero had dined centuries before listening to the cries of the Christians burnt alive, the Vatican. Jesus and Christianity were now Romanised.

To expect the population of the Roman Empire to translate to Christianity overnight was an unrealistic demand, with Constantine allowing both sets of religions to operate without penalty. Christianity was formally the state religion, knitting together the East and West as one with its spiritual thread.

Facets of Roman paganism were, however, retained within this new Christian faith. The worship of goddesses was compensated by the importance placed on the Virgin Mary, the mother of Jesus, the Madonna, with the cult of the vestal virgins translating to nuns, females devout to Christ, virgins for life.

The panoply of gods was compensated by the sequence of saints, all with individual traits of importance, to be worshipped on set days of the year, and with basilicas set aside for them. Sunday, the core day of Roman worship, was declared a holiday, replacing the Saturday as the Sabbath for the Christians. The cult of the Sun God, formerly worshipped on the Sunday that was now Christian, was replicated in art with halos adorning images of Jesus, Mary and the Saints.

The emperor himself remained ambiguous in his worship and beliefs, purposefully so, erecting an obelisk in the new Circus Maximus with Sol Invictus, the Invincible Sun God, inscribed next to his name.

The Christian basilicas were adorned with statues of Jesus, Mary and the Saints, replacing the idols of the Roman panoply, with Christ on the cross. For the first time, the image of Jesus was being fashioned, not in the image of a Jew, but a Gentile, drawing on the tradition of Greek busts depicting bearded males with long hair emerging from acanthus leaves symbolising death and immortality.

The church of Christianity was now named Catholic, meaning global. For Christianity was the global religion of the Roman Empire, Judaism at its roots, with the spirituality of love and physical abstention inspired by the Greek philosophers, and the signs and symbols and superstitions of Roman and Greek paganism. Roman Catholicism was the synthesis of them all, contained within a political structure led by the High priest and the Emperor Constantine himself.

But what of the original Christians, persecutions gone martyrdom no more? Rather than the trappings of Rome they retreated to their newly found monasteries to lead a life of dedication and asceticism, in silent protest. Their faith of spirituality had been drowned by the new state religion of Christianity festooned with paganism.

"Take these gold and silver vessels; go and put them in the Temple in Jerusalem, and let the house of God be rebuilt on this site" Ezra

5 The Book of Devils

The Catholic Church embraced the depictions of Hell from the pagan tradition of Rome, with the Devil an instrument to scare the Empire into conformity and belief.

300 years before Constantine's conversion Virgil composed the Aeneid, drawing on the mythical traditions of Rome's founder Aeneas, its centrepiece a trip to the Underworld. The demarcations of Hades unfolded before Aeneas, an area for those who committed suicide, encircled by Styx, unable to find rest; the homes of the blessed in the land of joy, amid fortunate woods, scented bay trees, soft river banks, and fresh streams; and an arena of eternal torture for the wicked racked on the wheel, Tisiphone with her scourge, a monstrous hydra with 50 black throats, Phlegyas beneath a teetering rock, Tantalus starving before a feast.

This was the vision of Hell that the Church of Rome now wished to portray, with the full pagan horrors of Devils, demons and torture for those who failed to comply with the new state regime of Christianity. The Devil and Hell were set for a wave of pagan embellishments, captured by art on the Basilica frescoes, and, centuries ahead, in the Vatican itself, Michelangelo's depiction of God's judgement in the Sistine chapel, with its depictions of demonic horrors in the descent to Hell.

The early Christian perceptions of the Devil and Hell were far gentler, almost unmentioned, certainly less pronounced than

Michelangelo's art. Satan in the Old Testament scriptures was no horned beast with a pronged trident to torture, but a son of God, who questioned faithfulness, the Satan that in the New Testament tested Jesus in the desert for the forty days of fasting, tempting him to turn stone to bread to break his fast. It was only in the final book of the Bible, Revelation, that the Devil had taken shape and in a vision at that, a great red dragon with seven heads and ten horns.

The notion of a torturous Hell was barely touched upon in the scriptures. The Old Testament location of the resting place for the dead was the innocuous Sheol, a place of shadows. Judaism was the survival of the tribe, not the destiny of the individual soul after death, certainly no Heaven or Hell.

Allusions to punishments after death were mentioned only for the extreme, for the king of Babylon in Isaiah for sending the Jews into Exile. His penalty was no eternal torture of rack, fork and flame, but a difficult descent to Sheol, his soul finding no rest until he arrived. The new Christian spirituality evolved with an after life, living with God in Heaven, or in torment in Hell. Jesus in the Gospels mentioned Hell just once, the agony of flames in his story of the rich man and his punishment in death for failing to help Lazarus the poor.

John's book of Revelation saw Heaven as a holy city, a New Jerusalem like jasper, clear as crystal, where God resided with His people. Hell in contrast was a lake of fire and sulphur, inhabited by the Devil, a place of torments day and night for ever. But these were visions, in a book of allegory.

In the new Catholic Church, however, the Devil and Hell were now the focus, aligned with Virgil's visions of eternal torment for the souls of the pagan wicked. The brutal psychology of Rome, with its sword and Coliseum of gladiators and torture had intervened. Pagan and Christian were integrated, an effective instrument of the new political control of state Christianity, the Devil to scare Christendom into conformity and belief, Hell as an instrument of control.

*"And the Devil who had deceived them was thrown into the lake of fire,
and they will be tormented day and night forever." Revelation*

6 The Book of Politics

**The Nicene Creed was composed, the oath of allegiance not
only to Christianity, but also to Rome, with those who dared
question the Bible's composition sent to the fires of Hell for
heresy.**

Following Constantine's conversion, toleration towards
Christianity was mandated across the Western Empire. The
progress made in philosophy, mathematics and science, and
wider advance in human psychology accompanying it, had
rendered worship of the pagan gods all but redundant, with
Christianity there to fill the vacuum at the emperor's bequest.

By AD 313 Christian toleration was Empire wide, with the
path towards Constantine's absorption of power in the East ten
years later made that much easier, as the architect of this new
religious tolerance. Constantine's reward in AD 330 was the
renaming of Byzantium to Constantinople. Byzantium was the
gateway between East and West, the centre of potentially more
trade and even greater power than Rome itself. Constantine duly
transferred his seat of power from Rome to Constantinople,
thereby setting the foundation for the new Byzantium Empire
that, as history would reveal, would outlive Rome by a thousand
years.

Theological control of Christianity by the imperial
government was now essential. The Council of Nicea secured
this. With Jesus declared fully divine the priests were formerly
empowered with the blood of the divine Christ at Holy

Communion. Anti heresy legislation was passed, with appropriate sanctions and punishments for any dissenters. The publication of the Nicene Creed was the fulcrum of this new legality, a document summarising the core beliefs of the state Christian faith that all members of the Roman Empire needed to both understand and keep. Its opening words, 'I believe in one God', formed a pledge of allegiance to one Empire under one emperor, with God alongside.

The newly elevated role of the Virgin Mary was confirmed in the Creed alongside belief in the holy Catholic Church itself, with the remission of sins dependent on one baptism. With Roman Citizenship now dependent on baptism, forgiveness for sins from God had become contingent on being a citizen. The Nicene Creed achieved nothing other than to make Christianity and citizenship one and the same.

Within this context, formalisation of the Bible was essential, what books to include within the Old and New Testaments. The Jewish scriptures were already defined. But the New Testament was far more open to choice. A third of the books considered for inclusion were removed, including a number of gospels, the gospel of Philip, for example, for its suggestion that Jesus had a sexual relationship with Mary Magdalene; this would have brought into jeopardy the claim that Jesus was fully divine, and have undermined his focus on the spirit over the body. The gospel of Mary Magdalene was also excluded; the Roman Empire was firmly patriarchal with Paul in his letters confirming the silent role of women.

A whole range of 'Gnostics' scriptures, the secret teachings of Jesus exploring the nature of God and salvation, were also excluded. By the end of the exercise, stamped by Athanasius of Alexandria, 27 works were included.

The most important decision of all was the inclusion of the Jewish scriptures themselves, the Old Testament, with the early Christian writings the New. The Bible started with God's creation, and finished with Revelation, the replacement of this world, with God's new Heaven and earth. The combination ostensibly made sense, looking rounded and complete. But the combination was internally divisive, theologically at odds, dangerously contrived, and as it was to prove a book of power for the politicians, one that could destroy.

The Old Testament was about the tribe of Jews looking for territory, with God on their side, their ultimate force in battle, victor against their enemies. God was the God of the Jews, and no other races. The Old Testament was also about kingship and state religion. All of which would have appealed to Constantine.

His emperorship could mirror that of King David, with Roman law given by God, he the Messianic human to ensure its implementation. At the same time he could appeal to the more spiritual nature of the New Testament with its promise of afterlife for those following the law, now synonymous with the rules of the Roman Catholic Church. Beyond which, he had at his disposal the threat of eternal fires in Hell for those who failed to follow Roman law, and the precepts of the Roman church. Given that the New Testament in the writings of Paul also affirmed that all political powers were God ordained, the Emperor was affirmed as spiritual leader, God's regent, divine.

But Old and New Testaments were not cohesive in their theologies. The New embraced all nations, the Old only one. The New was pacifist, the Old a book of war. The New was based on internal spirituality, the Old an external show of religion, Temple based. Above all, the New was based on choice and freewill, where the individual could choose to believe or not.

The Old was a rule book for society, where those who failed to comply were the enemy. On all counts, Constantine would have favoured the Old. For Christianity was firmly back in political territory, Judaism Romanised, with an afterlife to incentivise, and eternal Hell as punishment for those failing to comply. Those who refused to include the Old Testament were soon to be persecuted, burnt alive for their dissention.

"Let every person be subject to the governing authorities" Romans

7 The Book of Popes

The church survived the fall of Rome becoming the one surviving thread of communication across war-torn Europe equipped with its growing web of monasteries.

The marriage between the Roman Empire and Christianity lasted for just one hundred years, with Rome falling to the Visigoths in the early fifth century AD. Roman supremacy that had dominated the Mediterranean world, stretching from England to Egypt, Portugal to the Persian borders was at an end. Roman Catholicism survived, however, despite being held to account for Rome's fall. The days of the Roman Emperor were over, but not for the pope and Roman Church.

But first the soul searching of what went wrong, given that the Christian Empire, where God had worked through the agency of both Empire and emperor, had failed, Roman supremacy collapsing in its wake. In the aftermath, Augustine, a bishop, composed the City of God, in reaction to scholars who were arguing for a return to paganism, and blaming Christianity for Rome's fall. Politics, he argued, needed to be divorced from religion, theologically neutralised. Augustine wrote of two cities, Earthly and Heavenly. The Earthly City could participate in lust, power and money under the political leaders. But Christians within it could also look forward to the afterlife in Heaven with their internal hopes, faith and love directed towards this end. Christians could use the resources of the world to exist externally while living in the spirit and looking forward to the afterlife. Non Christians in the mean time could continue to enjoy the world in its own right.

Augustine had turned the clock back, drawing on the scriptures themselves, with focus once more on an internalised faith, soul rather than body focused, and less on the political participation that Catholicism had come to represent. Augustine went further speaking against the former political system where the emperor had been in charge of both church and politics. Instead, he argued for a straight split with the temporary world of politics left for the politicians to manage, with the Heavenly world, or City of God, led by the pope as Peter's successor, disciple of Christ.

In line with this, the Catholic Church focused on the religious communities, monks and nuns leading austere lives of devotion and prayer, soul over body, disciplined and physical abstemious, seeking daily their absolution from sin. But rather than looking inwards, the Church of Rome, in line with the writings of Paul and his message of evangelism, sought to spread its influence and the gospel message far and wide.

With the fabric of the Roman Empire gone, the onus of spreading the message across Italy and beyond was on the church itself. With the armies and legions of Rome disbanded, there were no supply lines and communication to support. Embedded in the memory of Rome and its papacy, however, was knowledge of the earlier empire, its geography, its people, its resources, and retained within its psyche was the capacity to organise.

With the political power of Rome in shreds, and with Europe sinking into internal warfare, the Church began to fill the gap left by the imperial void by transporting its Christian message Europe-wide. At its extremity lay England largely pagan following the fall of Rome. The method employed by the 6th Century monks to infiltrate was the same as across the rest of Europe, the allure of trade and connections. Europe was in disarray, with the Roman Church the only surviving thread of communication between the warring nations, the currency of cross border recognition.

The church could read and write in an increasingly illiterate world, equipped with knowledge of what was going on elsewhere across Europe with its vast monastic web. Signing up to Christianity had clear commercial benefits for King Ethelbert of Canterbury, not least the stronger cultural link that this would give him to the powerful kingship of France. The King of Northumbria followed suit, with Roman Catholicism reasserting itself across the extremities of Europe.

For a brief period during the eighth century, Charlemagne, King of the Franks, re-ignited hopes of imperial recovery. Whole sections of Europe were united under his leadership, with the Church of Rome firmly on his side. On Christmas Day AD 800 the pope proclaimed Charlemagne the new Augustus, a rival to the Byzantine Empire. This was what the Roman church had long been waiting for, a super national force to match its monastic spread, military might to support its spiritual influence across Europe. But such hopes proved premature, with Europe slipping back into internal warfare on Charlemagne's death.

"For everything there is a season, a time to break down, and a time to build up" Ecclesiastes

8) The Book of Arabs

While Europe descended into power struggles, the Arabs united under Islam and advanced across Africa to Spain and north via Jerusalem to Turkey.

The Arabs lived in the remoteness of the desert, the Persian Empire on one side, the power of Rome on the other, distinct groups worshipping their own gods. Mecca was their prosperous trading centre between India and Syria, with wealthy traders, and feudal groups fighting over the spoils.

All this was set to change in the seventh century AD, with the rapid spread of Islam, a new religion to unite the Arab lands, territory and influence expanding in its wake. Military successes were initially achieved in Syria, Palestine, Egypt, and Iraq, with the leadership, the Caliphs, spreading the story and message of Allah their god, and Mohammed their founder to the wider Arab world.

Mohammed lived in Mecca in the early seventh century, witnessing first hand the wealth creation, the in fighting that accompanied it, and the plight of the poor. He retreated to the desert where over a number of years and living in a cave he wrote the Qur'an, the words of Allah communicated to him, the new faith of Islam. Mohammed returned to Mecca with his divine revelations, but was repudiated for his belief in Allah. He left for Medina instead where he became governor, meeting with political and military success along the way. On his death in AD 632 the Caliphs, his deputies, began their wider mission for Islam. When Jerusalem was conquered by them in AD 637, a celestial golden dome was built on the site of the Jewish Temple, specifically on the rock where Mohammed, according to Islamic tradition, had ascended into Heaven.

Islam was an expression of Arab unity, and growing confidence, in the wake of the collapse of the Roman Empire, and increasing Arab wealth. By the time of Charlemagne's reign in Europe in AD 800, the nation of Islam had expanded massively, stretching along the African coast right into Spain, Baghdad its cultural centre. Vast swathes of the former Roman Empire succumbed to Islam, including Jerusalem, the former Jewish capital, and city of Jesus' Resurrection, symbolically displaying the golden dome. Bounty from the invaded lands was the primary goal, rather than the spread of Islam itself. Locals were free to engage in their local affairs, beliefs and customs, provided they paid their taxes to the Muslims. Jews were respected for their religion.

The faith of Islam itself was built on the Five Pillars. Belief in one God, and reverence for the Qur'an underpinned the need for Arab unity. Sharing with the poor addressed the imbalance of the nation's wealth, with the fast of Ramadan instilling respect for food and potential excess. Praying five times a day disciplined the faith, with the once in a life time pilgrimage to Mecca giving the nation a geographical centre, with the prayer mat and mosques, all facing Mecca, becoming the soul's compass. Islam meant submission, with its followers the Muslims those to submit. The Arab tribes had successfully combined their traditions customs and beliefs all united under Allah, with the Arab nation submitting to this new faith.

What Judaism was for the Jews Islam became for the Arabs, local desert gods replaced by the one God of Israel, local Arab gods replaced by Allah. The essence of Judaism lay in its Ten Commandments, of Islam in its Five Pillars. For law the Jews had the Torah, the Muslims the Shariah, effectively the rule of government. Feasts and celebrations held the communities together, the Passover for the Jews, the feast of Ramadan for the Muslims. The Jews were one united family under God, the Arabs one united nation under Allah. Core to each was belief in God, the identity and faithfulness of the nation, an invisible presence with idolatry a capital offence. Both faiths claimed Abraham their ancestor.

Islam also drew on Christianity, the core figures of Jesus and Mohammed each ascending into Heaven, affirmation of the afterlife. Islam for the Arabs, however, was more than just a reflection of Christianity, it was its perfection. The New Testament scriptures focused on the personal and spiritual connection with God outside of religious hierarchy. Islam was the same with Muslims allowed direct access to God on a prayer mat, clerics not required. The difference, however, was in the role of state; Christianity according to the New Testament texts was able to operate outside of it, whereas Islam was core to it. Islam was a religion that offered a personal relationship with Allah but in a framework of government that was both the state and the religion. It was closest to Constantine's Christianity, where state and religion worked together, with individuals pursuing their own spirituality within this framework.

The Caliphs of Medina spread the story of Mohammed and his teachings to the wider Arab world, with worship of Allah, the Qur'an, and the Shariah, all leading to further victories, and spread of Arab influence. The former Empire of Rome in the mean time failed to re-establish, engaged in internal warfare, while the Arabs looked to the nation as a whole and continued their expanse.

"These are the descendants of Ishmael, Abraham's son" Genesis

9 The Book of Crusaders

Pope Urban II ordered a holy war to combat the growing Islamic threat to Constantinople, granting remission of sins for those who participated.

In AD 1095, Pope Urban II received an ambassador from the Byzantine Emperor asking for help against the Muslims. The response to the request was overwhelming, with an army of 60,000 knights and peasants whipped up into patriotic fervor to crusade against the Muslims by the rhetoric of the pope and his catholic establishment. 'It is the will of God' was his motto, one that was repeated by recruiters to the cause Europe wide. Motivations were various. Muslims to the Church were pagans, with stories abounding of Christian pilgrims being attacked maimed and killed by them on their way to Jerusalem. There were also the practical considerations, the risk of Constantinople being attacked, with loss of trade; worse still, of the Byzantium Empire falling, the final buffer against the Muslim East. Sending a united army of crusaders would also have benefits for home, internal fighting among the European nations replaced by an external fight against Islam.

Pope Urban II was a prince ready to take on the world. His vitriolic against the Muslims at the Council of Piacenza secured the crusade, with the Christian armies challenged to re-take the holy city, and the church of the Holy Sepulcher within it.

The power and influence of the Catholic Church came into its own, with Pope Urban declaring the crusade a 'holy' war with remission of sins for the crusaders. This was the currency they could not refuse, the barons, knights and their infantry, forgiveness for all previous transgressions. The Devil and Hell remained core to Catholic belief. The promise of an afterlife and removal of the threat of Hell in return for a trip to the East to kill some Muslims and take Jerusalem was too much to resist.

For over a year the crusading force marched, their initial assault a nine month siege of Antioch, the cradle of Christianity. This was the city where a thousand years earlier the gospel writers had composed their stories of Jesus, a man of peace, the initial inspiration behind the Christian faith that now led to unspeakable carnage inside the city as the defenses broke.

Finally, three years into the crusade, Jerusalem was taken, Muslims and Jews slaughtered in their thousands, men, women and children, the killing all justified by the remission of sins. The crusaders were a deranged force, starving men, delighting in their tortures, boiling Arabs alive in pots, cooking children on spits to eat, a cannibalistic frenzy according to accounts from the time. The crusaders gathered in the church of the Holy Sepulcher in the city where Jesus had been tried and crucified, secure in their remission of sins, rejoicing in their capture of the holy city.

A thousand years before, a Christian message of love and compassion had formed in this same Jerusalem in answer to

Rome, a society based on the sword and crucifix, the brutal oppressor. The new Christian sect was compassionate, pacifist, with afterlife the victory. The Crusaders had achieved their victory, and secured their afterlife, but were nothing more than Roman soldiers of old, slayers with swords, perpetrators of execution. On this occasion, however, the ultimate voice of command was not that of a pagan emperor but of a Christian pope.

Following success in battle, a sequence of crusader states were formed throughout Syria and Turkey, taxed by their new European barons, wealth flowing back to Catholic Rome. Pope Urban II died before learning of the crusade's success, but his wider goal was achieved, removal of the Muslim threat to Constantinople, relative peace at home, and an Empire in the East.

Discord was set to return, however, with the Arabs rallying behind Saladin, and a second crusade that ended in defeat. Kings, knights and barons, Richard the Lionheart in their midst, united for a third crusade, but with victory limited to the port of Acer, unimportant to the Muslim cause. Finally, the ultimate disgrace; the fourth crusade attacked Constantinople instead of Jerusalem, in response to a request from the Venetian traders hoping to secure more trade routes with the East. Although against the pope's wishes, the outcome was the same, the slaughtering of fellow Christians. The crusader armies had abandoned all ideological pretence, returning to the traditional cause of war, wealth and trade.

The four crusades reflected the violent energy that drove both politics and religion at the time, a drive to find a common enemy to attack and unite warring factions at home. Christianity and Islam initially formed the banners, later Catholic versus Orthodox, the shirts worn to determine enemy and foe.

The conflagration between Muslims and Christians was eventually resolved, at least in terms of territory, with the Muslim

Turks taking Constantinople in AD 1453, some 350 years after Pope Urban II had instigated the first crusade.

The Ottoman Empire formed at the end of the thirteenth century spanning South East Europe, the Middle East and North Africa, now had Constantinople as its centre, with Constantine's Byzantium Empire in the East finally succumbing to Islam. In turn, the Christians descended south into Spain into Muslim territory, ousting the Arabs and Jews.

"You may, however, take as your booty the women, the children, livestock, and everything else in the town, all its spoil" Deuteronomy

10 The Book of Confessions

Following the failure of the crusades the pope fell into disrepute, an impotent force in the face of science, learning, and nationalism ignited by Luther's claims that the Church of Rome was a corruption of Christianity.

In the wake of the victory of the First Crusade, the papacy in Rome was at its pinnacle of influence, its seat a palace originally owned by the Emperor Constantine. The pope was on the throne, the emperor himself. 600 years after Rome's fall Rome had resurrected in the form of the Catholic Church, empowered to excommunicate kings, and raise armies to fight super states.

Nor did the Catholic Church hesitate to use its new found power, hunting out the heretics. Papal forces slaughtered the non catholic Cathars in France for believing that power stood in the way of love. Monastic inquisitions with torture were instigated, those confessing burnt at the stake. The Grand Inquisition followed in Spain to rid the country of Jews and Muslims who had previously converted to Christianity, heretics lined up ready to be burned, one last chance to repudiate their views, and then set alight. Popes nodded and kings executed, all part of God's plan.

The papacy was now just one remove from the pagan emperors of old watching the blood and gore entertainment in the Coliseum, the power to determine life and death, Virgil's depiction of tortures in the Underworld, and flames of Hell, resurrected by the pope himself.

Despite which the papacy cracked. Money and wealth were becoming more important motivators than control of religious sites, the diversion of the fourth Crusade from Jerusalem to Constantinople symptomatic of this trend. Trade and money brought new divisions, with city strife taking its toll. Dante wrote his visions of Hell, inspired by these bloody times, with Dante blaming the corruption and weakness of the pope himself. The papacy even fought itself. In 1377 the seat of the pope returned to Rome to its new headquarters at the Vatican from Avignon, France, leading to two contenders for the papacy, one in France and one in Rome, the pope and antipope.

This was the period of renaissance, publication of fine art, and scientific discovery.

The writings of the ancient Greek philosopher Aristotle were once more being studied, man a political animal, city life not church his ultimate fulfilment. Science was an additional threat. In God's scheme the earth was the centre, circumnavigated by the sun itself, with Galileo called before the Roman Church to repudiate his theories that the earth circled the sun.

Nationalism was the greatest threat of all. Sovereign states were beginning to emerge, equipped with new religious ideologies. The German monk Martin Luthar translated the Bible, and used the original texts to demonstrate that the pope's claim to infallibility that had allowed him to order the holy crusades and in more recent years grant remission of sins for vast sums of money had no foundation in the Bible at all.

The Church of Rome could no longer hide behind the obscurity of its Latin texts. Equipped with such newly found wisdom, with Bibles translated into native tongue, the nations of Europe were on the verge of clawing back religion and faith for themselves, protestors against the superstitious and idolatrous practise of the pope and his catholic masses.

"Better to obey God than man" Acts

11 The Book of Monarchs

England united under the Tudors, with its king, Henry VIII, monarch supreme over state and church, no longer prepared to take orders from a pope that failed the test of biblical scrutiny.

When man became king, the king aspired to God. In AD 100 the Emperor Hadrian refurbished the great Temple of Zeus in Athens, with a colossal statue of himself erected at its side. With Zeus the father of Greek gods, it was clear where Hadrian saw himself, in relation to the Empire he ruled, an icon of divine presence on earth. Emperors aspired to deity, and killed Christians for refusing to acknowledge their divinity. Although the Catholic Church detached from such pagan perceptions, the pope still claimed infallibility as God's voice on earth, a descendent of Saint Peter himself.

As the powers of nationalism grew across Europe the draw of divinity proved too much to resist for the kings of the realm. England was emerging from decades of war between the rival nobilities of York and Lancaster. The bloodshed had reached its climax at Tewkesbury, with the fighting spilling into the cathedral itself, the nobles of the defeated House of Lancaster lined up in the cathedral grounds for their beheading. The Tudors that followed, however, achieved stability as descendants of both blood lines, with Henry VII, the first of the lineage. Epiphany was chosen for his coronation day, the church's celebration of the kings visiting the baby Jesus. The Crown Imperial was placed on his head, a crown jewelled like non before it, effectively Jesus crowned king. Like the Roman emperors before him, English kings were aspiring to deity.

Henry VIII succeeded to the throne a few years later. Initially Henry was a papal supporter, the most Christian of kings in the eyes of Rome following his military intervention against France whose king had been threatening to attack the pope. Henry subsequently wrote The Defence of the Seven Sacraments, a book that earned him the title Defender of the Faith. When, however, the pope questioned his authority a few years later on an issue of morality, and blocked his right to divorce, not only did he withdraw his papal support, he banished the Roman Church from England altogether.

Henry as English monarch of a unified and increasingly powerful nation was no longer prepared to take direction moral or otherwise from the pope, quick to seize on the arguments of Luther that the papacy was flawed. Paul's letter in the New Testament to the Romans vindicated his stance, with God the authority behind all political appointments. Henry as a king appointed by God could now demand absolute obedience from his subjects, monarch of the Cities of God and Earth one and the same, supreme in state and church, with the archbishop of the new Church of England, his spiritual lieutenant, to support and advise.

Henry prayed in church, listened to his conscience and made his pronouncements, claiming God for himself. Subjects had a choice, to be with God and king, or be pronounced a heretic worthy of torture and execution, the hideous and prolonged death of hanging, drawing and quartering. To be against Henry was to be against God, a sin demanding death. Henry ordered the execution and sent the traitor to his maker, to face God with his own conscience and guilt.

For centuries feudal kingdoms across Europe had happily deferred spiritual guidance to Rome. The power of Rome and its pope had grown to heights usually enjoyed by imperial powers, equipped with crusader armies, conquerors of Jerusalem, slayers and torturers of any who questioned their authority and law. Now, a thousand years on from the fall of the Roman Empire, and the rise of the Roman Church in its wake, the nations were claiming back power one by one across Europe for their own, national heads of state and church, God king and country in unison.

As supreme monarch in England, appointed by God himself, Henry could now set the rules to suit his own agenda. This he did, destroying the monasteries, taking their treasures and wealth for his own. Anti Catholic fever gripped the nation, with the pagan elements of Catholicism laid bare, the statues of Christ, Mary and the Saints, the idolatries forbidden by Moses, stripped from the churches. Confessions to the priest were banned. Most important of all, the Bible was published in English, with Henry's portrait on the title page larger than that of Christ himself. Henry had claimed God for his own, ruling the country at will.

"But if you do what is wrong, you should be afraid, for the authority does not bear the sword in vain!" Romans

12 The Book of Divisions

Kingship of divine right was destined to failure, with the growing levels of wealth and understanding of their subjects demanding a greater role for government.

The outcome of the Reformation for the noble families across England and the population at large proved bloody and tortuous. Henry's son Edward, during his brief period as king and before his premature death at 15, was even more ruthless in his application of the new Anglican faith, in his role as Christ's vicar. All adornments in the church buildings were removed, with the wall paintings of saints whitewashed, and the altars removed. Any who objected, rebel forces in the West Country, were crushed by the army.

Queen Mary, Edward's successor, reverted to Rome, sending 300 or more Protestants to the agony of the flames, the Archbishop of Canterbury, Thomas Cranmer, one of them. Schizophrenic swings in enforced religious practise were proving difficult for the manor communities to bear. Subjects of the English monarchy had a choice; share their religion, or risk charges of heresy and death at the stake.

In response, Elizabeth on her accession adopted a middle way. Church services reverted to Protestant ideology, but kept their Catholic traditions, with many of the church adornments and festival days of saints reinstated. People could worship in the way they had for centuries before the Reformation, provided they recognised that the English monarchy was now head of the church, not the pope.

Attempts to reinstate Catholicism would continue through the following century, Guy Fawkes' attempt to blow up parliament the most infamous, with James II losing his crown because of his Catholic sympathies. Despite which Henry's achievement of displacing Rome as the head of religious authority over England was maintained. Like many nations across Europe, control of religion had returned to geographical boundaries, reflecting stronger national units. The imperial might of Rome and its evolution into Christendom had finally left the shores of England one and a half thousand years after the first military incursions of Roman soldiers under the leadership of Julius Caesar.

In nationalising religion, Henry had established a monarchy more powerful than its predecessors, bordering on deity. Inadvertently he had also set the foundation stone for the Christian faith to break from kingship control in the centuries ahead. For the translation of the service and the Bible into English that Henry had facilitated had made the Christian faith more accessible to the people as a whole, had empowered them with knowledge that had previously only been in the remit of the monastic communities. With wealth patterns changing, the growing class of merchants, and later industrialists, were making increasing demands for government checks on the levels of power held by the king.

The path to secure the change would initially involve bloodshed. Cromwell attempted it first by raising an army. The civil war that followed led to the toppling of the monarchy and the execution of Charles I. Cromwell enforced a puritan approach to Christianity, with all vestiges of Catholicism removed, the celebration of Christmas and the singing of hymns banned. Religion had gone from one extreme to another, from pomp and ceremony and divine monarchy, to austerity and military rule. Cromwell's puritanical approach was equally disliked, with the monarchy consequently reinstated.

What followed was a gentler and more evolutionary process, with divine kingship replaced by a government of ministers. The peaceful replacement of pro Catholic James II by the Dutch protestant William of Orange and Queen Anne towards the end of the seventeenth century was the final repudiation by government of absolute monarchy based on divine right. The monarchy was retained as Head of State, and Head of Church, but with power massively reduced settling into a more symbolic role, a stamp of approval for decisions already debated and taken by Government.

Despite which monarchy continued to be a strong force of religion, almost the religion itself, in later centuries, with the relationship between God and King maintained by the monarch's symbolic role as Head of Church. The monarch was prayed for in church, sung for in the National Anthem and sanctified at the coronation. At Elizabeth II's crowning in 1953, Westminster Abbey resounded to Handel's choral masterpiece Zadok the Priest and Nathan the Prophet harking back 3000 years to the moment that King Solomon of the Jews was anointed king. The religious connection between the monarch, its people, and a hidden divine force of appointment had survived, even if the monarch ruled no more.

"And all the people rejoiced" Handel

The Revelation of Spires

The people celebrated the mystery of God's love regardless of such political change, kneeling before their vicar, and worshipping God.

The people gathered in their churches to praise God, worship their king, and bow their heads in prayer. Superstitious practices had gone; the statues and symbols of paganism replaced by effigies of Christ on the crucifix for their forgiveness, statues of the Virgin Mary his mother for their devotion, and portraits of the saints for their inspiration. The land was Christian, kings and lords worshipping God and Jesus, priests administering forgiveness of sins, monks living lives of austerity, all aspiring to God's love and holiness for an afterlife in Heaven.

In prayer and devotion they entered Gods' church. Outside the barons and kings waved their flags on horseback, claiming God to be their own, equipping them with swords to fight and conquer, the Messianic kings of old, to achieve glory in battle, and an afterlife with God in Heaven. The people believed, inspired by the words of priests from the mystery of Latin texts, by the sanctity and holiness of the church, and by the message that they were all fallen from the grace of God.

They celebrated the cycles of the year, just as their pagan ancestors had done but with God at the core, darkness at All Souls, the turn from darkness to light at Christmas, spring at Easter, high summer at Ascension. The cycles of life and death, baptism and funeral, and marriage were all there at the church. The people gathered to hear their hymns, life's joys and sorrows reflected, victories and defeats, and within them God's love and compassion, sombre and uplifting. Hymns were loved; the source of music for courage and affirmation, comfort in times of despair.

The church gave morality and the people listened; the Ten

Commandments enshrined and read from the lectern, forgiveness offered for those who had transgressed, sermons issued from an elevated stand close to the altar. The people looked for spiritual guidance from their pews, words inspired by God. They listened to the biblical laws, Moses on the mount receiving them directly from God himself, the priest to ensure their deliverance.

The Bible was recited at baptism and marriage with words of hope and blessing, and was read at the funeral to comfort. For each and every occasion there was a Bible passage, a connection with Heaven, God's will revealed. The Bible in hand gave authority to witnesses in the court of law, the judges pronouncing sentence, and the vicar with the criminal waiting to be hanged.

The Bible affirmed the king, and the state, and the military commanders ordering the attack. Biblical verses were learnt by rote at the schools, strewn on walls, boards and signs and memorials for the dead for all to see. The Bible was God's will, the fount of Heavenly wisdom, inspired by God for his people.

The people looked up to the spires pointing towards God and upwards to Heaven, and walked through the churches paved with the graves of their ancestors of old, monuments to lives that had gone before, the knights and warriors that had fought so bravely for God, the nobles, and their king. They heard of Moses and the Egyptians drowned, David and Goliath slain, Daniel and the lions tamed, and Jesus resurrected from the dead. They listened to the vicars preach, of the wickedness of the body and purity of the soul, of the dangers of the Devil, and obedience to society and reverence to the king, of God's love and holiness. The people believed, and followed their king and aristocrats embracing the Bible through life unto death.

"We humbly beseech thee bless our gracious Queen Elizabeth " Church of England Book of Common Prayer

Testament 1111 The Individual King

The separation of religion from politics and the reaction of the individual to their new found religious freedom

The books

1	Missions	5	Choirs	9	Charismatics
2	Trenches	6	Mirrors	10	Therapists
3	Monuments	7	Kings	11	Genes
4	Revolutions	8	Merchants	12	Churches
Revelation	Charis				

Tensions caused by the industrial revolution unleashed warfare and political upheaval on an unprecedented scale.

The traditional political system of God, king and country was replaced by democracy with the individual in society at last empowered to choose religion or ignore it altogether.

The majority were no longer prepared to bow to God the stronger force, with governments adopting the role of the compassionate in response, pandering to their needs.

The church was left by the wayside slow to react to the moral revolution that accompanied such change with literal belief in the Bible challenged by politics and science.

A wider spirituality was required to satisfy the search for human meaning and purpose.

The spirit of 'Charis' displayed in the New Testament, the grace of human behaviour, was the Christian hope for the Third Millennium.

1 *The Book of Missions*

Christian political theory justified the exploitation of newly found territories to fuel the industrial age.

With the Old and New Testaments taken together kings and politicians had long been able to justify their actions by choosing the passages of the Bible that most suited their purpose. The religious prism of the Bible had endless ways of directing the light to satisfy their agendas. The king could be the New Testament peace maker but could also claim God as his own as he was about to order his troops into battle. The slave traders could cite the Old Testament laws to justify their beatings of the slaves, while the African slaves looked to the inspiration of Moses to set them free. Proponents of the death sentence could call on the Old Testament's tooth for tooth, and salvation in Heaven for the soul purified by its execution, with those against it citing Jesus' spirit of forgiveness. The Government could choose elements of the Old Testament law as God's will, and ignore others, in the spirit of the New Testament's broader definition of ethics. Tyrant kings in the mean time could do as they pleased equipped with Paul's statement that kings were God ordained.

The Bible was certainly used to support the removal of other faiths. When the Spanish armies swept through South America in the sixteenth century, all but destroying the indigenous tribes and their customs, the pope via the military explorers was simply fulfilling the demands made by Jesus to his disciples just before his ascension to Heaven, 'to go into the whole world and proclaim the good news to the whole creation'. The obliteration of local customs and tribal beliefs by the invading forces was simple fulfilment of God's command, with the destruction of Mayan texts, and dismantling of the Aztec and Inca traditions obedience to his word. The acquisition of huge levels of treasures and wealth that would have accompanied such indigenous destruction would, of course, not have gone unnoticed to the popes and kings of Europe, the 'incidental' advantage.

As far as the European explorers were concerned, the indigenous tribes of America were nothing more than barbarians, savages who participated in heart sacrifice, who flayed their enemies, and wore their skins as spoils. The Christians kings and pope back home by contrast were civilised, with their own instruments of torture, and public executions at the stake and gallows necessary to ensure Christian observance and maintain a civilised society, with Christianity the very definition of civilisation. The outbreak of small pox and typhus that destroyed 80% of the Aztec population within 60 years of the European arrival was simply taken as God's hand in their subjugation.

The political doctrine of European Christianity in any case demanded the removal of local traditions of religion. Subjects of the realm were answerable to the king, the pope and finally to God in Heaven. If the conquered races of the Americas failed to recognise the Christian God of Europe, they were by definition failing to recognise the political authorities represented by their European acquirers.

Centuries before the Jews had suffered their own imperial oppression, with the Roman soldiers ousting Judaism from Jerusalem, razing their Temple to the ground. Christianity had evolved as a spiritual response to such Roman brutality, designed to operate outside of political regimes. Yet Christianity was now the very imperial force obliterating customs and religions of American tribes as precious to them as Judaism was to the Jews.

The industrial age of the eighteenth and nineteenth centuries demanded even greater levels of international exploitation to satisfy the growing need for resources and labour. In line with the compassionate message of Jesus, the church provided education and medicine, and above all salvation with the prospect of eternity in Heaven for those converting to the Christian faith. This was the cloak of righteousness worn by the politicians and their armies while the vast continents of Africa, India and beyond were raped of their resources and people. For the wealth of the world was now magnetised towards Europe, with Christianity the justification of the pull and Britain the centre of its pole.

"Proclaim the good news to the whole creation" Mark

2 The Book of Trenches

The industrial age was built on hard work, discipline, and social and moral codes, all biblically based.

The industrial revolution of the nineteenth century transformed Britain, with huge building works and structural advancement, the urban revolution, accompanied by mass migration from the country as people sought to improve their lot. Hard work and ambition could lead to wealth, with the emergence of a new middle class. But for many, the opposite held true, with squalid conditions, poor sanitation, high mortality rates, degradation of the human condition.

Victorian society was family as they believed God would have wished, with morality based on biblical texts. Queen Victoria and Prince Albert were the devoted couple, produced many children, and formed the icon of family life. Man owned his wife, and took her assets, with woman a servant to her husband, who in turn was servant to God. Divorce was the Devil. Strict discipline was society's ethos, in the schools, the workplace, and most of all the workhouses provided for those who had failed the Victorian dream. Soul over body was the Victorian bedrock, Christian based, derived from God. Destitution was akin to immorality, with the poor deserving their fate, while the wealthy were closer to the king and therefore to God. Society was breaking at the seams, with the city streets lined with the destitute poor, gutters and rivers overflowing with sewage, factories and mines maiming their workers, wives and husbands trapped in loveless marriages, the elderly locked in workhouses, children working the mills, opium addicts seeking their fix. But the nation thrived, and the Bible held it together, family and class structures kept in place according to God's will, a strict moral code of endurance and obedience enforced in line with God's law. Marriages lasted, despite the torments, and workers endured despite the dangers. Society went to church to pray, following God's call for physical abstention and social order. Beneath the surface of opulence enjoyed by the few, the wealthy land owners and captains of industry were the poor enduring hardships of labour and shocking levels of poverty, with no voice to defend. The owners maintained their stranglehold of control, with church and religion alongside, supportive of the class and hierarchical structures. At the base of Victorian society was physical and emotional suppression, like a huge industrial coiled spring, set to snap back and reclaim the Victorian development with its own wave of destruction.

The nation aspired to greatness, an empire four times the size of Rome, with Queen Victoria, donned in black, the icon of austerity to achieve it, the grand matriarch of Europe. Her grandchildren were its leaders, the British King, the German Kaiser, and the Russian Tsar. Landlocked Germany was jealous of the British and Russian Empires, with all three soon to be drawn into conflict on a scale the world had not seen before, the family that had once inspired the Victorian ideal now the feuding family of Europe. The nationalist fervour created by the prospect of European war was welcomed by its nation's leaders. War was embraced, preferable to the lurking threats of civil discord and work force rebellion.

The process of Victorian industrialisation that had led to great feats of civil engineering, heavy iron constructs and machinery powered by explosive power were suddenly turned against its people. Workers and owners alike were now lined up in trenches dug by the civil engineers, equipped with heavy iron killing machines, weapons of explosion, mechanisation to kill and slaughter. Urban construction turned to human mutilation, as the armies sought to kill and destroy; humankind in a war greater than all before. Aristocratic generals planned the attack, gentrified captains blew their whistles of command, and the working class rank and file leapt over the ramparts, all mown down by enemy fire, all following the call of God.

"To die for one's country is honourable and glorious" Horace

3 The Book of Monuments

Social order determined where people sat in church and where they were buried, with obedience to God, king and country driving them all to war.

Churches long ago had been financed and built by the nobles, their purchase for Heaven, with the peasants encouraged to attend. Effigies of the knights and tombs of the aristocrats were placed close to the altar, impressive stones to record their significance; the paupers were buried in the outer remits of the church yard, a small cross to mark their place; in life as in death the rich and the poor.

Absolute monarchy had been disbanded. Heresy was a torment of the past. But social hierarchies remained, with the churches reinforcing them, the vicar from the aristocratic ranks maintaining clear boundaries and dividing lines. Pews were marked for those of social importance, the workers gathered at the sides and rear. Entire communities attended church, clothed in Sunday 'best', top hats for the aristocrats, cloth caps for the workers, seated in the pews and buried in their graves according to their class. The church service underpinned social standing, prayers made for the monarchy and the government as a matter of course, hymns praising God and King.

The country and its structures were synonymous with religion itself. St Pauls was the nation's Temple, boulevards across London reaching towards this hallowed centre, its Vatican like dome towering above the City, with architectural splendour and internal decor rivalling Catholic munificence. The Christian nation gathered in St Pauls to celebrate victories over their enemies in France and across Europe, and honour their military dead. Tombs and effigies recalled their great military leaders, Nelson and Wellington, war gods for the nation, the dead of the military forces and their tombs lining the crypt.

At the outbreak of the Great War in 1914, God king and country all conspired to recruit soldiers for battle. The role of church offered its divine backing, and that special sense of duty instilled by the church service itself, the officer classes paraded in the pews at the front, the privates at the rear. In the summer of 1916, half way through the conflict, soldiers emerged from the trenches in line with military command, marched across the open fields to be slaughtered in their thousands by enemy fire.

Prayers said at home for their safety were replaced by funerals for the dead, the church that had encouraged their enlisting now conducting the burials. Memorials to those who had died in glory, obedient to God king and country, were erected, names listed according to rank, social structures reinforced to the end.

Remembrance Sunday commemorated the end of the Great War, with uniformed members of the community in attendance, the forces, the medics, the nurses, the scouts, the guides all saying their prayers for the dead and prayers for peace. They gathered in front of the stone listing the glorious dead, the crucifix of Jesus above it. Jesus according to the New Testament scriptures had died a painful death, painful as any in the Great War, punished by the Jews for questioning the religious authorities of the day. Jesus was a pacifist, promoting an internal spiritualism based on love and compassion in the face of Roman oppression and brutality.

Jesus was non hierarchical, the first last, and the last first. Yet Jesus on the crucifix today was surrounded by the hierarchies, in military uniform, with a priest to conduct, the war dead remembered by those that had requested their conscription. Stretching back to Constantine's conversion at Mendip, Christians had been embroiled in military action, participators of political might and instruments of the state, with the individual spirituality of early Christianity swamped by politics and imperialism. The Great War marked its pinnacle.

"The rich man in his castle, The poor man at his gate" Cecil Frances Humphreys

4 The Book of Revolutions

Sustained political upheaval ousted God from politics.

In Tudor England under Henry the king ruled with the rack and gallows. Kings were divine, monarchy absolute, God and king ruling the people. Increasing levels of trade and commerce led to a new intellectual force of wealth and influence. A government of aristocrats replaced the king as ruler, with the king the rubber stamp, God the framework of moral reference. The industrial revolution that followed created a third layer of influence, the workers. The aristocracy and church held them in restraint, and then unleashed them into the battlefields of The Great War, nation against nation.

Millions were killed, and millions maimed, with the ruling combination of aristocracy and church questioned in its wake. Trust in the ruling classes had been broken, blind obedience of the workers lost, God for some removed from the political equation altogether. The people wanted power for themselves and to be rid of the structural collusion between the aristocrats and church that had sent them to the factories and squalor and to war and death.

Russia responded with communism. The Tsar owned the country, while the peasants starved, and then faced slaughter in the Great War, the enemy ahead, the Tsar's army behind shooting the deserters. The people revolted, and stormed the Kremlin, the Great Palace, and the cathedrals of God that had supported him. God was banned, the State their new guiding force, the papal authority of Rome, the Vatican and the Grand Inquisitor now The Politburo, Red Square and the KGB of Moscow. Communism was the state, the people and the religion, with torture and execution for dissenters, fear of Hell replaced by fear of the secret police, the Gulag and Siberian labour camps. God had gone, and the individual with it, replaced by conformity within the people at all levels, mind, soul, dress, wealth and spirit.

National Socialism, as an alternative response, began in Germany and swept through Europe, with Nazi forces pushing through France, Poland even Russia imposing their ideology on conquered states. The aftermath of the Great War had replaced God with the nation itself; individuality was denied, with the people the nation's disciples. Hitler their leader stood above them, greeted on stage by uniform cries of his name, Hitler and Victory one and the same, an imperial demagogue, a symbol of their advancement. Those who did not fit the nation, or could not lead its advance, were lower than human, outcasts, fit for labour and then for death, the Jews, the gypsies, the mentally impaired, the disabled. The nation was strong, strove for racial purity, and sought to crush those around it. The crusading armies of the pope had slaughtered those who would not convert; the Luftwaffe of Berlin bombed the cities of those who resisted the Nazi advance. SS guards hounded down the Jews, as society outcasts who looked to Jerusalem not Berlin, and sent them to Hell on earth, starvation camps for labour, medical torture and eventual extermination. The nation had replaced God, becoming God itself, its people collectively empowered.

The British and American forces led their assault across Europe towards Berlin, spurred on by Churchill's rhetoric, to defend their Christian values, the Christian world of individual freedom at war with the totalitarian world of National Socialism. The Christian church was packed with congregations praying for the safety of their soldiers, and the salvation of their individual liberties from the Nazi regime. Communities pulled together under the shared threat of aerial bombardment and Nazi invasion, with the church at the centre for this support. Vicars recited the New Testament beatitudes, for the meek and the persecuted, the peacemakers and the mourners. Hymns were sung to lift morale, 'Fight the good fight'. Prayers were said for the dead, valiant in their cause.

Democracy triumphed, the Nazi regime falling in 1945, communism collapsing in 1990. Europe was reunited 75 years after the initial outbreak of the Great War, free of totalitarian influence. Political systems that had crushed the individual were gone, but also the older aristocratic systems that were supported by religion. Across Europe God and the church were now distanced from politics, with religion a matter of personal choice. The relationship between aristocratic government and the Christian church had finally come to an end, God king and country no more.

The path had been long, painful and bloody; two world wars, and a number of political revolutions. The aristocrats had been displaced along the way, and the working classes now had a voice of their own in the new wave of European democracies, one that sustained individual freedom outside of totalitarian regimes. The human cost to get there had been unfathomable, but society finally settled into a fairer more equal system of politics. The unsustainable social pressures that had built up in Victorian society had been resolved, and for the first time since Constantine's conversion in AD 306 politics and Christian religion were now independent forces across Europe.

The motive that had inspired thousands of young men to serve in the Great War, God king and country, had merely secured its end, with the sacrifice of those fallen in the field of battle achieving something far greater than national glory.

Spiritual freedom for the future generations of Europeans had unwittingly been achieved.

"The Battle of Britain is about to begin. Upon this battle depends the survival of Christian civilisation." Winston Churchill

5 The Book of Choirs

With the individual liberated from religious restraint, youth was the first to break free.

Music was inspired by God, performed for kings, and reflected the moods of the nation. Plainsong chants reflected chastity, and were sang by monks in their quarters, sonorous in spirit, sober in body, the monastic tradition that had lasted for centuries. The age of national kingship matched by papal decline demanded more tunefulness and dance, the minstrels parading the Tudor courts of Henry VIII, an expression of passion and belief. Society turned inventive, mathematic and scientific, captured by the classical works of Mozart and Bach, ordered in rhythm. The industrial revolution that followed was matched by the baroque compositions of Handel, more complex in arrangement, multi layered. The romantics wrote their works inspired by the Victorian age of expansion and opportunity. Each era sang its song, with the church and cathedral concert halls there for the performance, God and kings in attendance to hear.

Music was collective, orchestras under the command of the conductor's baton, military bands on the march. The big band music of World War II reflected the comradeship of the air squadrons, the daring spirit of their pilots captured by its swing, the deep throat sound of fighter planes mimicked by its brass. Music had always reflected the group agenda of government, military leadership, divine kingship, and its people.

In the decades of peace that followed World War II the tempo of the music suddenly changed to rhythms and sounds not encouraged by the government or by the church. The infiltration of rock music was sudden, its energy evolved from black slave music. Its fast pulsating beat encouraged moments of violence as youth danced to its rhythm. Structures of society were outraged, the teachers, the politicians, the church leaders at this new subversive influence, the music of the Devil outside of church or political control.

Rock gave youth the voice to break free from their slavery view of society, parents, church and government, restrictions to their growth and expression. For the first time in humankind, youth said no, with society powerless to respond. Youth rebellion in the Jerusalem of David, the Rome of Caesar, or the London of Henry would have been dealt with brutally, with stoning, Crucifixion, the execution of a heretic. Now, en masse, youth questioned the foundations of government, their motives for war, with music their song and voice to express.

The majority of the world had lived in slavery, subservience and squalor, while the rich had lived in decadence, their leaders motivating tribes and Empires to go to war, and finally the world with religious fervour, the banner of God. Now the earth itself was threatened with global destruction with democracy in the west and communism in the east engaged in a cold war of nuclear intent. Society wanted change with youth empowered to express it.

The medium for its expression suddenly turned to The Beatles, working class, irreverent, their music upbeat, lyrics affirmative, a compound of yes and love. The scream of youth was deafening as crowds gathered in music halls, lined the streets of cavalcades, crammed into airports, to hear the Beatles perform, watch them move, see them breathe, worship them as gods, honour them as kings. They sang and strummed guitars, affirming their love and youth. The crowds worshipped and wept, and formed their deafening screams, the collective shriek of youth breaking free, the chains of church, government, kings, and God, and their forces of suppression, execution and war finally thrown aside, a primeval yell ascending to the Heavens.

2000 years before a new spiritual phenomenon had swept through the Roman Empire, Christian-mania, the voice of love and compassion, a reaction to the brutal suppression of Rome's military might, and oppression of religious groups, its followers prepared to die. Within 200 years the message had spread to the extremities of the Empire, motivating the emperor himself to embrace it for his own. Beatle-mania took less than a year to spread the globe, accelerated in its spread by newsreel, radio, television, and mass musical production, without the threat of martyrdom on discovery. The power of the forces was the same, refreshingly innovative, non-political, love based following decades of discord, war and hate.

The energy soured, with darker lyrics, with yes replaced by no. Youthful optimism had been greeted by a world that remained violent, where the leaders failed to listen, where young soldiers were being conscripted for battle, mutilation and death, Americans sent to Vietnam to fight for political ideology. The music of experimentation, Eastern spirituality, and revolutionary anger that followed in rock's musical progression reflected a world where its youth had woken up beyond the screams and were demanding change in a world where its leaders were forcing the innocent to engage in acts of violence and death.

The Beatles were now more popular than Christ in the words of Lennon its founder. Based on active attendance at church, where numbers had plummeted compared with the meteoric popularity of the Beatles, his observation was as powerful as it was alarming for the clerics. Christian fanatics responded with public burning of Beatle records and their effigies, execution of the group for heresy.

Lennon was a modern day Socrates or Jesus, no longer walking the streets of Athens or Jerusalem, but New York and Washington questioning the motives of government for war. His message was peace, delivered outside of political frameworks and social hierarchies. Candles were lit, his anthems sung, not in Jesus' Gethsemane, nor in Socrates' gardens beneath the Parthenon, but in Central Park, New York to celebrate his life at the moment of his death. Lennon was an individual with a voice that had been heard by a people that could now express itself, in a society where expression of spirituality had been set free.

"Free as a bird" John Lennon

6 The Book of Mirrors

Modern society had evolved, yet the church was unable to respond, lost in a moral maze of biblical mirrors, relying on texts reflecting societies 2-3000 years ago to justify their outmoded stance.

Tribes, nations, empires had their own versions of morality, reflecting the needs, aims and location of their groups at specific times in history. For centuries European nations drew on the Bible for their moral codes. Jewish law was full of specifics: for treatment of slaves, ownership of wives, ejection of lepers, avoidance of meats, stoning to death, all essential for the tribe to be healthy, strong and multiply.

The law was pragmatic at every level, with morality the customs to ensure best practice for survival. As societies progressed from tribal to national to imperial, best practice was bound to change with different needs and priorities for survival. Morality shifted as societies developed.

Christianity of the New Testament in contrast to Judaism was not a state religion, with a sequence of laws, but an internal way of living, living in the soul rather than the body, an ethical rather than legal stance. Paul's letters may have focused on the need for a physically abstemious life, to have sex only if really required, to avoid licentious and drunken behaviour, and to avoid homosexual acts, but they were not written as laws, legally proscriptive. Paul in his letters argued that Christians should obey the political structure of the time, with kings ordained from God. Christianity had been designed as an internal and spiritual way of living that operated outside of politics, with governments to be obeyed separately. Give to Caesar what is Caesar's.

The core to Christian living was the aspiration of neighbourly love. In the gospel writings Jesus had extended the boundaries for his neighbour from beyond the Jews to everyone regardless of race, relating the parable of the Good Samaritan, a society outcast at the time. With popes giving licence to kill Arabs, and kings of nations leading their men in charge against foreign armies in the name of God and king, in the Old Testament tradition, a clear confusion was taking place between Old and New Testament ethics, and which should be followed.

Morality throughout the history of the Bible's use to support it was in reality nothing more than the fulfilment of the interests of those who happened to be in power at the time, in varying levels of response to the needs of society. In line with Old Testament rules, the slave traders could beat their slaves provided they lived for two more days; a king meanwhile could have a wife, and many mistresses, and yet still execute his wife and lover for adultery. Those in charge set the moral tone, with the Bible a mirror maze of moral and legal application.

The moral values of Victorian England drew especially on Paul's New Testament ethics. With Victorian society based on formal marriages for the upper class, and forced labour for the workers in squalid conditions, Paul's spirit over body and mind over passion formed the perfect antidote. Soul over body neatly matched the work ethics of the mill and mines, long hours, tough conditions and little pay, to ensure a prosperous nation for the owning class. In line with the biblical texts, sexual modesty was encouraged, with acts of homosexuality a heinous crime. Marriage vows were to be kept, even if the motive for marriage had been wealth rather than love, with adultery a sin, for fear of bastard offspring that might drain the estate. Paul's New Testament ethics on sexuality suited the aristocratic cause perfectly.

By the late twentieth century Britain had transformed into a country based on democratic principles with equality of rights promoted between the genders. Social mobility and availability of contraceptives meant that sex could be enjoyed more freely beyond the confines of marriage, with females now enjoying the same property rights as males within a marriage. The trend towards cohabiting couples grew on the back of it. The breeding psychology of the nation also shifted, with the need to produce large families negated by improving mortality rates. Homosexuals enjoyed the same rights as heterosexuals reflecting these sociological shifts. With multiplication of the race no longer an issue rules for sex had transformed. The patriarchal society of the Old and New Testament, where the man owned his wife and could beat his slaves, was now redundant. The days of quietly submissive women as Paul had instructed in his letters were long gone.

The problem for the modern Christian church was how to accommodate and reflect these changes in its own moral code. Even if Christianity was no longer a state religion, the church was still required to give a formal view to its members. The difficulty remained as it had done for the Christian states centuries before, how to define the Christian law, which elements to retain from Jewish tradition and which to bring in from local practice. The default position for much of the twentieth century was to retain the Victorian principles, the traditional family values, sex within marriage only, homosexuality banned. The church grew increasingly isolated because of it.

The church was trapped by its doctrine. Insistence on following any of the Old Testament laws was greeted by charges of inconsistency; if the church maintained its ban on homosexuality, it would also be free to reinstate slavery and throw the sick outside of the city. If on the other hand Paul's letters in the New Testament were to be followed, sex would be discouraged, and females would be silenced altogether.

The Jewish Law reflected the society of 3000 years ago, New Testament ideology 2000 years ago. Society of AD 2000 had changed inexorably, no longer slave based, no longer patriarchal, and no longer needing to multiply in case of plague, war or famine. The clerics, bishops and archbishop gathered to debate morality, gay vicars, and women priests lost in a moral maze of biblical mirrors, current law and accepted social practice.

"The ruling ideas of each age have ever been the ideas of its ruling class"
Marx and Engels, The Communist Manifesto

7 The Book of Kings

Society was now comprised of individual kings, with the state pandering to their every need, providing the compassion.

From working the fields, sitting in the pews, and donning their caps to their aristocrat owners, individuals drove their cars and owned their homes, travelled overseas, and sought their pleasures. They knew their rights; bosses, teachers, the police, even the country's leaders all showing reverence, subjects in the court of the individual kings, scared of being sued.

Individuals stopped going to church. The concept of a God in Heaven, behaving like a king in court, requesting glory, favours, prayers of forgiveness, with the threat of Hell if displeased, seemed as abhorrent as a Tudor king sending his subjects to the gallows for execution. Kneeling at the feet of a god in his court, with hands together, head bowed, in supplication, where the king could strike at pleasure or feel benevolent and forgive, was a million miles from where the individual king of society would stand today. The individual was God himself, with the state at his command.

Politicians pandered to their needs, and answered for their actions. The newspapers performed the inquisition, the new popes of Rome, hounding those who stood in the way of the individual's march to power, monarchs who showed disrespect, politicians who failed their targets, teachers who pushed too hard. The councils performed the administration, ensuring safety at every turn, steps that were not too steep, air that was adequately clean, chairs that supported the back, scared of the individual king.

Individuals basked in their glory, bullying their way through crowds, loud on their mobile phones. Society was theirs, for their promotion, pleasure, service, wealth, and personal fulfilment, individuals with family and a court of friends, the police their guards, the teachers their servants, the politicians their donkeys, the newspaper to ensure all behaved according to their will. Society had become a collection of individuals with power to sue, tell on the police, report the teachers, and execute their dismissal.

Individuals had knowledge, able to read, to click the web, the library of the globe.

For centuries the Bible had been their source of knowledge, wisdom and spiritual enlightenment. Now they tested the thesis, questioned the teacher, and scrutinised the priest, discarding the Bible, and leaving the church, agnostics, atheists, converts to other faiths. For centuries men had lined up in battle dress, obedient to God and king, ready to kill, prepared to die believing in the after-life and a place in Heaven. Now they believed in the current life, living it today and maximising its pleasures.

The children were princes, had everything they demanded and did as they pleased. They bullied their parents, dictated to their teachers, and patrolled the streets, authorities with child command. They sat in their homes, the frustrated energy of a young individual, displaced and angry.

The early Christians 2000 years before had responded to the brutality of Rome with an internal spirituality based on love and compassion, with blessings and salvation for the poor, meek and hungry. The state persecuted while the individual believed in God, Jesus and love, and looked forward to an after-life in Heaven. The early Christians lived in the spirit looking beyond the pleasures and pains of this world ahead to the next. Now the roles reversed; the individual the persecutor, the state granting compassion. With this the only life to live, the individuals lived for themselves, for wealth, pleasures of the present, and power over other individuals, with the state to provide the safety and compassion for those who suffered its harms.

The country's leader was no longer a king, a tyrant who would kill at will, but was compassion himself, head of the nanny state for a society of needs. The sick, the poor, the disabled, the hungry, the unemployed, all demanded the state to provide.

The state was saviour to the individual kings; a safety net for their physical and emotional needs. The sick and elderly were no longer parked away in the workhouses but nursed in hospitals and homes. Racial minorities were no longer mocked as outcasts but given equality and respect. The disabled and mentally impaired were no longer hidden from view but embraced with privileges and care. Criminals were no longer judged and condemned for ever, but served a sentence and then rehabilitated. The early Christian message of love, compassion, equality and acceptance, the beatitudes of Jesus in his sermon on the mount, was no longer being aspired to by the individual, but by the state itself. State religion had gone. The state had become Jesus instead.

Individuals were charitable, collecting money for the disadvantaged, doing good deeds for the community at large, some quietly and with goodwill, others as individual kings, advertising their works and receiving the glory, self aggrandisement.

The Pharisees in the New Testament parable prayed loudly and noisily gave of their wealth, while the widow quietly gave her mite. Society was full of self promoting kings creating great charitable commotions, proudly and loudly doing their giving, seeking the charitable label, and masking their sins.

The state had become Jesus, the individual a king, and God was gone. Individuals no longer aspired to Jesus and God but gods of individual idols, those who excelled in their fields, the sportsmen, the pop stars, the dancers, the writers, the business men. This is where people wanted to be, on the stage, with an audience, divine in their fields, fame and glory once enjoyed by monarchs now enjoyed by the individual, gods themselves.

"How hard it is for those with wealth to enter the kingdom of God"
Matthew

8 The Book of Merchants

Individual kings pursued their greed to levels that threatened to destroy the economic system that had once empowered them.

The popes of Rome lived in imperial splendour in palaces once owned by Constantine himself, English monarchs, heads of the church, in castles owning the wealth of the land. Yet Jesus according to the gospel writers had entered Jerusalem on a donkey without a possession in the world, claiming it to be easier for a camel to pass through the eye of a needle than for a rich man to enter Heaven. Christianity according to the New Testament scriptures was focused on living in the spirit, and storing up treasures in Heaven, not the accumulation of wealth on earth.

For the Jews of the Old Testament, the wealth and prosperity of the nation as a whole was what was important. The Jewish scriptures were aware of the risks of individual wealth within the tribe, and disallowed the charging interest on loans between members of the tribes as a consequence.

Empires and nations that subsequently adopted Christianity operated differently, with the king the embolism of the nation; the wealthier the king, the wealthier the nation. The greed of kings always sought its justification. Christian monarchs focused on the messianic status of David in the Old Testament living in kingship splendour rather than Jesus the desert wanderer, and their divine appointment by God. Popes played the custodian role of the Christian riches acquired to glorify God, with the pope part of the glorification itself. Societies were structured according to what those with the power could get away with, Christian or not; the weaker the people, the richer the king.

Money lending was initially prohibited among the Christians, in accordance with the Old Testament scriptures forbidding lending at interest between brothers, with all Christians deemed as brothers in Christ. The Jews filled the gap. Although they could not lend to each other, they could lend to those outside of the tribe. Their reputation as sharp money traders had been sealed since New Testament times, with Jesus' fit of rage at the money traders in the Temple followed by his betrayal for cash by the Jewish named Jude.

Following their eviction from Jerusalem, the Jews lived on the fringes of society, performing the vital function of money lending. Monarchs and popes preferred the Jews to operate the banks if it meant that their subjects remained outside the banking practice itself, and not get rich themselves. This relationship with the Jewish bankers may have been one of mutual dependence, but it also fuelled resentment among the residents of the countries in which they operated given the wealth that the Jews might accumulate for themselves. Pogroms were commonplace across Europe partially because of it and culminated in the systematic killing of the Jews in the Nazi death camps. The bankruptcy of Germany following the Great War created the excuse, with the Jews blamed in their role as traders, forced to wear stars of David painted yellow, the colour of Jude the traitor. There was also a deeper reason on this occasion and one that fuelled the hatred. The Nazis as part of their political regime and ideology aspired to their own perfect race, with Jews an intolerable presence as a consequence, given their claim as God's chosen.

Greed accompanied power. The king had absolute power and so kept everything for himself, until the traders gained wealth and increased their power at the expense of the king. Two kings were beheaded, Charles in England and Louis in France, monarchs reluctant to let go of their divine status, and trappings of exorbitant wealth that accompanied it. The cycle of greed continued with the aristocrats exploiting the labour of the poor to increase their industrial turnover and financial returns. This in turn sparked new uprisings across Europe, two world wars, revolution and political turmoil.

Greed would always be the force that threatened the political system.

By the end of the twentieth century democracy was firmly established across Europe, a free market economy, where hard work and effort regardless of class, race and gender could lead to wealth and opportunity. It was now the turn of the individual kings to find their greed fired up by the politicians to own their homes, invest in shares, manage their pensions, and gain their financial freedom. Business men and bankers pushed to the limits of what could be achieved, operating in a culture of return where growth meant higher rewards. Jews and Gentiles alike, the financiers were now the cream of the individual kings, with their leverage genius creating a bubble that was threatening to break the very economies on which they were based.

If democracy were to break under the greed of the individual king, God would no longer have the option of returning to the state; totalitarianism had already failed with its own destruction. Nor could God go back to the combination of state and church, with the consequences of state religion appearing too evil to the society of individuals that had now discovered religious freedom. Society could only move forwards to a new plane, for compassion to rest more equally between the individual and state driven by individuals free to choose their own spiritual path.

"for your merchants were the magnates of the earth, and all nations were deceived by your sorcery" Revelation

9 The Book of Charismatics

The charismatic movement of Christian evangelism evolved with its own quest for personal salvation and individual king significance.

As state and religion separated, religious sects formed all claiming the gospel their own, teaching the Bible, proclaiming God's word. The charismatic movement dominated these sects with a message of personal salvation; Jesus died on the cross to save the sinners, with eternal life for those who believed. Evangelicals shared God's love and message of salvation seeking to save those around them, promoting a moment of personal salvation, one in which the sinner could be transformed by the power of the Holy Spirit.

Charismatic Christianity, like all other church movements and sects that had gone before, reflected the times in which it was formed. Society had turned permissive, with individuals within it seeking immediate highs from drugs, sex and rock 'n' roll. Charismatic Christianity responded with its own spiritual fix, the moment of conversion, God entering the soul and filling the emptiness of the individual with his transforming love. The evangelical logo, 'Smile, Jesus loves *you*', appealed to a modern society of individuals seeking purpose and meaning with the offer of a personal relationship with God. Christians shared the moment of their conversions with fellow Christians, their moment of fame and significance on the Christian stage, as they gave their personal testimony.

Leaders of the Charismatic movement stood on podiums in the stadiums normally frequented by pop idols and sports stars, spoke with passion, and invited all to come forward and receive the spirit of Jesus, speak in tongues, shout his glory and feel the high. All over the land, charismatic preachers stood up, delivered God's message of love, and basked in the emotional response, the audience singing Alleluias, prostate on the ground in submission to God's wonders, beneath the preacher's arms of deliverance.

Like Paul in the New Testament, Charismatic Christians all had stories of personal encounters with God, and interpretations of scripture. God had spoken to them all in person, and they all had messages of spiritual wisdom to share. Charismatic Christianity was full of individual kings keen to share their message, write their book, build their chapel, and influence their flock. They claimed God for their own, gifts of his spirit, and were on a mission to bestow the love of God to those around so desperately needing salvation.

Evangelicals focused on the moment of conversion, when the individual made the choice, from a life of sin to one of salvation, born again. Charismatic Christians were self proclaimed as saved, destined for Heaven because they knew God's love, individual kings set for eternity in Heaven. But what of those who did not convert, those who failed to get the message, those who lived prior to Jesus' ministry, those who lived in the wrong part of the globe unable to get the message? Love God or be punished for eternity.

"Those who believe in him are not condemned" John

10 The Book of Therapies

When individual kings became depressed they confessed to the psychotherapists not the priest

The New Testament promoted the spirit at the expense of the body. Life was brutal under Rome with the early Christians retreating to an inner spiritual sanctuary, away from the cruelties of physical life, focusing on the soul striving towards God's goodness and love. The early Christians were prepared for martyrdom as a consequence, a willingness to endure extreme physical agonies and death, knowing that an after-life with God in Heaven was the reward.

When the Roman Empire seized Christianity for itself under Constantine, the relative importance of the soul compared to the body, and the promise of an after-life worked to the advantage of the politicians. Popes and kings could send armies into battle, with soldiers slaying their enemies, inspired by their promise of God's forgiveness and an afterlife in Heaven. If the pope and king were disobeyed not only would there be physical tortures in this life, there would be Hell and eternal damnation in the next. The political authorities and industrial owners could justify hard labour and toil for their workers as part of God's plan to purify the soul. It was considerably easier to control people if they believed they were sinners.

Society of the late twentieth century had moved to a very different place, with God and state no longer in congregation. People expected safety in the work place, and not to march to war. Striving for God's forgiveness, remission of sins, and Heaven and Hell were no longer tools of political control. The body of the individual, its safety and nurturing were now the responsibility of the leaders. Control and abuse of the body and the threats of a fiery furnace in Hell belonged to the kings and popes of the past, not the political leaders of today.

Individuals engaged in their pleasures, now that the shackles of political oppression had been lifted, with the process of guilt removed. People could live life with abandon, with the indulgence of kings, eating and drinking to excess, having sex with as many partners as they pleased, surrounded by personal trainers, life coaches, and make-over artists to serve their needs.

Pleasure was bountiful, fulfilment sometimes more allusive. Energies previously required for hunting and survival, defence and attack, were spiralling high but with dreams and aspirations that often fell flat. Testosterone turned inwards, with anger and depression on the back of it. Like kings in court bored with being king, the individuals summoned the psychotherapists and unloaded to their shrinks.

Psychotherapy was individual focused, in line with early Christianity. Like Jesus in the New Testament scriptures the psychotherapist was not there to judge, but to heal. Growth was the goal, and moving on, letting go of past hurts, the 'forgive and be forgiven' of Jesus 2000 years before. Unloading without reserve to the therapist facilitated the path, the confession of sin to Jesus.

We were all human, according to the psychotherapist, all fallen from grace said Jesus. But we needed to love ourselves because of it, the message of God's love in the New Testament. Love yourself first, then you can love others formed psychotherapy's core, the 'love you neighbour as yourself' of Christianity. 'God loves each and every one of us' claimed the Gospels, the regaining of self worth through therapy, a path towards spiritual intelligence and awareness, prayerfulness and awareness taught by Jesus.

Two millennia separated the teachings of Jesus, and the era of psychotherapy. The gospel essence of love seemed so close to the therapeutic process of healing the hurt and lonely, lost in their pleasures and aspiration. Christians drew on the beatitudes of Jesus and trained their own therapists providing counselling services for those suffering from depression and loneliness, confusion and grieving. The counselling that they offered and words of understanding that accompanied it were living works of Jesus' teaching 2000 years ago, a witness to his message of love and compassion.

There were differences of course, and challenges to overcome. Modern psychotherapy recognised the need for a healthy body as well as a healthy soul, a symbiosis of the two. Paul's teachings in the New Testament were somewhat different, promoting the spirit over the body, with disdain for physical pleasure even sex. 2000 years had passed, society had changed and the psychology of sexual behaviour with it.

Elements of Christianity were beginning to embrace this change treating homosexuality and divorce with the same love and acceptance as Jesus had displayed towards the adulteress when she had been caught by the scribes and the Pharisees and faced stoning.

Christianity was moving to a more open plane of love and acceptance. Christian elements that remain enmeshed in the literal readings of Paul continued to lose their support, priests replaced by psychotherapists where the church felt unable to move forward.

"'Let anyone among you who is without sin be the first to throw a stone at her.'" John

11 *The book of Genes*

Science had revealed the flaws of Genesis; Christians resorted to metaphor for truth with scientists aspiring to the creative force of God himself.

The Holy Bible was read from the lectern, God's holy word, the primary source of knowledge, the fount of truth. The king, the nobles, the leaders all gathered to hear its wisdom, the armies and peasants with them. All believed; none had any reason to doubt. The earth was flat, with the Heavenly stars above, fixed in the sky. God made them all, the fish, the birds, the animals, and finally man, in God's image, God the Creator of all things. Those who suggested otherwise were burnt alive in the streets of Rome. Galileo was quick to repudiate his scientific theories when he was shown the instruments of papal torture. Scientists learnt to keep their silence.

Not even the pope could stand in the way of scientific

progress in the centuries of industrialisation that followed, with biblical truths crushed under foot. God did not 'create' man as Genesis dictated; humans 'evolved' from primates, from fish, from tiny organisms, the seeds of life. God did not create the world in six days; dinosaurs inhabited the earth millions of years before. God did not even create the Heavens and earth; matter exploded as a big bang thirteen billion years earlier, spreading through the void with the earth finding its location as part of an infinitely larger process. For the first time in centuries people had a free choice, without the threat of torture or flames to goad them, to believe in the literal account of creation in Genesis or the scientific version of events that discredited the literal truths of the Bible.

The church was in crisis. The validity of the entire Bible, not just of Genesis, sunk under its weight, with God as portrayed in the Bible now under scrutiny. The Victorians initially reacted to Darwin's evolutionary theories with a new layer of imagination to soften the blow, belief in a world of fairies and the paranormal, the ability to contact the dead via mediums.

Time passed and non believers dismissed the Bible in its entirety, layer after layer of fabrication, with stories of a virgin birth and Jesus' Resurrection as far-fetched as God's six day creation. Those believers that kept their faith were forced between a literal read that contradicted these scientific findings, or a more metaphorical approach that led to its own difficulties of interpretation between metaphor and literal truth. If the biblical account of creation in Genesis was nothing more than poetic metaphor, why not the entire account of the life of Jesus in the gospels, a metaphor for a new spirituality?

The writers of Genesis had gathered in the courts of King David 3000 years before to finalise the Pentateuch, its mytho- logical account of early Jewish history. Genesis was a man- centric account of creation, with the hand of man writing it. God of Genesis had specifically created the world for man, for man to have dominion over every living thing that moved, with every plant and tree there for man's consumption. Man, according to Genesis, was the ultimate, the purpose of God's creation. God created light, water, land and the cycle of seasons in the first four days, the essential environment for plants to grow as food for the fish, birds and animals created in days five and six. Man was created on day six, with the sequence of all that had gone before there for no other purpose than to service his physical needs, man dependent on animals, dependent on the plants, dependent on the land, water and cycle of seasons, dependent on the initial light that God had created from darkness. God had turned on the lights for the fulfilment of one purpose only, to create man.

The evolutionary theory inspired by Darwin gathered pace. On a time line of earth's four billion years, man had only appeared at the thinnest sliver of time right at the end. Evolution was ongoing, with man changing form over the centuries, in physical stature and mental thought. Primate was a step to man, with evolutionary steps to continue, beyond the six day creation. The evolutionary process that had once cleansed the earth of dinosaurs would almost certainly destroy man. Further advances of life would take root and evolve, with mankind forgotten dust. The universe was evolving, with stars born and dying, planets energised by the stars and then consumed by them, with life forms and their cycle towards death permeating the galaxies.

The Genesis God had created the world and all of its resources for man, whereby he could be multiply and expand. Science suggested limits, however, detecting a cycle of decay caused by the bountiful consumption that Genesis had so forcefully advocated. Eco-friendliness questioned the Genesis God, with man a species like any other to be appreciated and protected, no longer the be all and end all of natural civilisations.

Science flourished and church attendance fell. To scientists the universe was a dispersal of energy from the moment of big bang 13 billion years before, with matter spiralling outwards, according to a dynamic pattern that mankind now sought to unravel. Scientists looked up to the Heavens, no longer seeing God, but the stars, and the light years of space that extended through the galaxies of light with probes and satellites seeking to unravel its mystery. The scientists on earth sought to unravel their own mystery of human life, how to sustain it, clone it, even create it, with the healing power of prayer promoted by the Bible being replaced by the penicillin pioneered by scientific chemistry.

God of the Old Testament, a man in the sky, had not created the universe in six days. Science had not yet resolved the source of the matter that gathered for the big bang, or the reason for its eventual displacement. Scientists had brains that could imagine multiple universes, but were unable to contemplate endless spiralling energy that seemed so large yet had no ultimate purpose apart from being. Man was finite and needed purpose, whereas the universe just was, finite or infinite. Science was striving to understand, to bridge the gap, to understand and control the universe and the forces that it contained.

Three thousand years before, the Jewish tribes had conducted their sacrifices and kept to their customs seeking God's favour. For the past two thousand years Christians had prayed to God seeking forgiveness for their sins in the hope of eternal life. Now the individual was God himself, deciphering the universe and its properties and forces, seeking their control. The mystery of the relationship between humans, their energy, and the energy of the universe that surrounded them remained, however. Science would continue to unravel this mystery of human connection, and Christians would call it God.

"Then God said, 'Let there be light'; and there was light." Genesis

12 The Book of Churches

Church buildings were losing their congregations, many crumbling into disrepair, symbols of political oppression from an age that individual kings would rather forget.

At every stage of society's development, tribal, imperial, national, industrial, religion was essential, the bind that tied the individual to the wider needs of the group, and granted obedience to its leaders. The popes, the kings, the industrial owners, the priests, the monks, the armies, the workers and the emperors were all part of a human evolutionary process of individuals learning to cooperate as part of a larger group and form societies. Each played their part, with human nature there to execute the compassion and cruelty, able to empathise yet greedy for more, able to love yet prepared to torture and kill.

The pope believed in his office, the emperor in Rome, the industrialists in financial return and the country's wealth; all believed they were operating for God and the greater good. The torturers and executioners for the pope and king were obedient and believed in the orders of their leadership. The dissenters and heretics believed in their scientific findings, and biblical texts, in a God beyond the authority of the pope and kings. All believed and all played their part in the wider evolutionary process of mankind. Empires came and went, nations rose and fell, kings ruled and died and their people with them. Yet the church and their buildings had survived these centuries of change.

In the new democratic age, however, politics and religion now stood apart, with the individual free to choose their own agenda, and the politician free to ignore. The church bells of Sunday rang out to a world of individuals, able to pursue their pleasures free from religious restraints, with the compassion of the cross, the celebration of Holy Communion, and the message of Jesus in the gospels and Christ in the letters of Paul lost on them. The churches were losing their congregations, with many of the church buildings beginning to crumble.

Beyond the shores of ancient Christendom, however, church trends were in reverse. Membership of the churches across Africa had soared, with the Pentecostal message of re-birth, healing and freedom in Christ, the perfect antidote for a continent suffering from political corruption verging at times on genocide. The Christian message of love and compassion fed the explosion with the churches representing freedom from political oppression. For unlike the ancient churches of Rome and England the churches of Africa were free of political control.

Churches across America were also growing with packed congregations. Many Americans chose to believe once more in God's literal creation as an antidote to the uncertainty caused by America's fall from political and economic grace that had accompanied the opening decade of the twenty first century. American churches had always operated outside of government control in accordance with the US Constitution. Americans had been free to choose their religion and beliefs, unafraid of external reactions that their beliefs might bring. The individual Christian in America could project with confidence, in comparison to Europe where centuries of controlled religion and execution for the heretics had driven the individual into spiritual hiding. America was a nation of religious self advertisement because it could afford to be.

The church across Europe was no longer under formal political control, yet still felt associated with it. There was still a Church of England, and still a Church of Rome. The pope continued to receive audiences with political leaders, and bishops in England continued to comment publicly though out the year on issues of national significance. The falling congregations reflected a people uncomfortable with any political connection to religion at all.

"We lift our hearts to the lord" – Church of England service

The Revelation of Charis

A wider spirituality was promoted, with the 'Charis' displayed in the New Testament offering the new antidote to the power and greed that pervaded modern society.

Throughout the ages the Bible had wielded its power, proclaiming God and salvation to those who read its pages. The Old Testament scriptures inspired the Jews to their salvation, surviving centuries of wanderings and geographic displacement until Israel's reinstatement in 1948. The New Testament inspired spiritual resilience, even martyrdom, among its followers with its message of love, hope and eternal life when faced with oppression. The Old and New combined formed the collective holy Bible, the foundation for state religion initially for the Roman Empire, then for Christendom and finally for the family of nations across Europe. Under its banner kings were crowned, societies were structured and people marched to death in war.

The Christian religion finally rested with the individual free to interpret its meaning or reject it altogether, framed as it was by the formal Catholic and national churches that had survived the dismantling of forced state religion.

Societies had evolved, reflecting the shifting layers of power and wealth, defining politics and the role of religion within it. Individuals evolved within these changes, no longer corporate members of a tribe, martyrs motivated by an after-life in Heaven, servants to the king obedient and loyal. Individuals were now their own masters, seeking their pleasures, scientific in approach, questioning the truth. Morality transformed alongside, reflecting the changing needs of society, women equal to men, homosexuality accepted.

Within all of these changes science and advancements in human understanding had made literal belief in the biblical message difficult to retain, obsolete for many. Neither societies

nor the individuals within it could go back to their former understandings of the world, equipped with blind belief in God, and
religious observance to secure his favour. Society had matured,
with the church and spirituality needing to follow suit if it was
to survive.

Individuals grew to adulthood and no longer believed in
Father Christmas, yet still believed in the spirit of Christmas
itself. Society was no different moving beyond a simple acceptance of God the almighty, Jesus the saviour, and eternity in
Heaven, searching for a wider spirituality, an understanding of
life, its purpose, and location in the wider universe.

God may not have been the almighty in Heaven creating the
world in six days and resting on the seventh.

Yet the mystery of the beginning of universal energy and the
cause of its displacement remained. Sacrificed goats were no
longer the answer, nor for many attending church and kneeling
in prayer. The unravelling of the mystery had become God, with
science its celebration, and humans the conscious energy to
reveal it.

Early Christianity had been inspired by a range of Greek
philosophies, as a philosophy itself, an individual defence that
responded to oppression with love. The New Testament writings
contained a message that had lasted through the ages, the voice
of love, compassion, hope and self worth in times of torment and
distress. Human greed and coercion surrounded it, imperial
forces of Rome, the guards of the pope, the court of the king, and
now the individual king himself, imposing his energy and will
on his frightened neighbour.

Jesus was the Messiah, the Christ, literally the anointed one.

Jesus was also the embodiment of Charis, the Greek word for
grace and loveliness, kindness and delight.

In a world where the literal meaning of the Bible was turning
figurative, Charis seemed easier to absorb, the embodiment of
the love exemplified by Jesus in the Bible, compassion for the

weak and disadvantaged. Charis-tians did not necessarily go to church, claiming God for their own. They did not even label themselves Charis-tian. They quietly aspired to God's grace, their interpretation of how to live as human, their connection to each other and the energy of the universe, their ultimate location and fulfilment. Biblical verses drew support for this, and church could be its location, with many within the church including its leaders already embracing its principles. Church after all was the space of spirituality that had been shared by centuries of ancestral leaders, kings and subjects, a place sure to welcome the individual kings of modern Christendom.

"I seek to honour the world in which I live, and marvel at its universal principles. I recognise what I need to live, to the avoidance of greed. I know my actions sometimes hurt others, and I let go of grudges. I strive for good, not evil. I aspire to a positive life of fulfilment, engaged in the wider energies of the universe" the Lord's prayer for the age of the individual king, Charis

BOOKS

O is a symbol of the world, of oneness and unity. In different cultures it also means the "eye," symbolizing knowledge and insight. We aim to publish books that are accessible, constructive and that challenge accepted opinion, both that of academia and the "moral majority."

Our books are available in all good English language bookstores worldwide. If you don't see the book on the shelves ask the bookstore to order it for you, quoting the ISBN number and title. Alternatively you can order online (all major online retail sites carry our titles) or contact the distributor in the relevant country, listed on the copyright page.

See our website www.o-books.net for a full list of over 500 titles, growing by 100 a year.

And tune in to myspiritradio.com for our book review radio show, hosted by June-Elleni Laine, where you can listen to the authors discussing their books.

mySpiritRadio